STATECRAFT AS SOULCRAFT

WHAT GOVERNMENT DOES

GEORGE F. WILL

A TOUCHSTONE BOOK
Published by Simon & Schuster, Inc.
NEW YORK

Copyright © 1983 by G.F.W., Inc., A Maryland Corporation
All rights reserved
including the right of reproduction
in whole or in part in any form
First Touchstone Edition, 1984
Published by Simon & Schuster, Inc.
Simon & Schuster Building
Rockefeller Center
1230 Avenue of the Americas
New York, New York 10020

TOUCHSTONE and colophon are registered trademarks
of Simon & Schuster, Inc.

Designed by Edith Fowler

Manufactured in the United States of America

10 9 8 7 6 5 4 3 2 1
10 9 8 7 6 5 4 3 2 1 Pbk.

Library of Congress Cataloging in Publication Data

Will, George F.
    Statecraft as soulcraft.
    Includes bibliographical references and index.
    1. State, The. 2. Conservatism. 3. Welfare state.
I. Title.
JC251.W53   1983   320.2   83-455

ISBN 0-671-42733-4
ISBN 0-671-42734-2 Pbk.

To Frederick L. Will
Philosopher

Contents

Well, then, a commonwealth is the property of a people. But a people is not any collection of human beings brought together in any sort of way, but an assemblage of people in large numbers associated in an agreement with respect to justice and a partnership for the common good. The first cause of such an association is not so much the weakness of the individual as a certain social spirit which nature has implanted in man.

—Marcus Tullius Cicero

Preface

ON THOSE infrequent occasions when readers want to confer a compliment on a columnist (or at least, on this one) they are apt to praise him for not being "predictable." What they mean is that there is an element of surprise, an unanticipated turn or outcome in what he writes. But a political commentator who really is unpredictable is a writer who is all sail and no rudder, and whose work reflects no discernible philosophy. When a kind reader calls me unpredictable, I am tempted to respond: To anyone sufficiently familiar with the minds of the Oxford Movement, *circa* 1842, all my conclusions are predictable.

However, the most frustrating aspect of a life of public argument is the assumption by the reading public that the arguer, because he bears a particular political label, must have a particular predictability. This gives a writer a dispiriting sense of being a captive of conventional—but inadequate—categories. It is not unreasonable for people to think that ideas come in clusters, like grapes. They think that if a person holds a certain belief, then he probably subscribes to certain other specific ideas—not because the others are logically entailed by the first idea, but because the others just seem, as a matter of custom, to come stuck together with the first idea.

Most politicians flee from political labels like "liberal" and "conservative," because the labels may circumscribe their political constituencies. But labels are reasonable, because a reasonable person's political judgments are not random. The familiar clusters of ideas manifest congruences and affinities that express political temperaments as well as political philosophies. Political ideas cluster; people cluster, politically. But there are moments, and this is one, when it is particularly important to suggest alternative clusterings. Specifically, the cluster of ideas that is commonly thought to constitute conservatism should be pried apart and reconstituted. This book is intended as a lever for such prying apart.

I am often asked: "Why do you call yourself a conservative if you believe" this or that? The question usually pertains to my belief in strong government, including the essentials of the welfare state. I will try to answer those questions here. I am not arguing that all intelligent persons of goodwill should covet the label conservative. I know many such persons who, amazingly, do not, which just goes to show that there is no accounting for tastes. Be that as it may, now is a good time to tidy up the idea of conservatism. Classifications should classify; they should include and exclude in ways that facilitate understanding. The classification "conservative" is so frayed at the edges that it is becoming an impediment to clear thinking and prudent government. My aim is to recast conservatism in a form compatible with the broad popular imperatives of the day, but also to change somewhat the agenda and even the vocabulary of contemporary politics. To those who are liberals and to those who call themselves conservatives, I say: Politics is more difficult than you think.

My primary concern is not with a theory, but with a condition. Inevitably, society is, to some extent, an arena where interested parties conflict and compete. But it is neither inevitable nor acceptable for a society to be, as ours increasingly is, an arena where big battalions clash by day and night. And yet that is apt to be the case when the public philosophy seems to license it by low expectations, and when public institutions seem unconcerned with the bridling of egoistic motives.

What follows is one person's persuasion, but a persuasion for all seasons. It is the distillation of two decades spent as a student and professor of political philosophy, a member of the staff of the United States Senate and a commentator on public affairs. These experiences have left me feeling moderate dismay about modern government, and somewhat more dismay about the likely long-term consequences of the philosophic assumptions that underlie the culture which modern governance reflects. So I have tried to strike a middling tone, between that of a tinkling cymbal and a firebell in the night.

CHAPTER ONE

The Care
of Our Time

> *Our country is not a thing of mere physical locality.*
>
> —EDMUND BURKE

IN A.D. 410, barbarians sacked Rome, and Augustine, a born pundit, reached for his pen. His aim was to defend Christianity from the charge that it was culpable for the calamity. The result was *De Civitati Dei*. When Saint Augustine picked up a pen, he didn't put it down until a large subject had been exhausted. Lest you be anxious, let me assure you that what I have to say is on a less exhausting scale. I have no provocation, aim or ability so grand as those of Saint Augustine. But my undertaking is Augustinian in two senses. First, I am concerned about the possibility of a kind of slow-motion barbarization from within of the few polities which are all that stand between today's worst regimes and the fulfillment of their barbaric ends. Second, to explain my concern, I must commit political philosophy.

I am a lapsed professor of political philosophy. But having become a commentator on public affairs, and a resident at the seat of the central government, I have a continuing, even a quickened interest in the state and standing of political philosophy. I subscribe to John Stuart Mill's distinction between "governing" and "controlling." A small cadre governs; the people control the governors. As regards the principle of representation, the people do not decide the questions: they decide who shall decide—their representatives. Thus "To get good government means to get consent to good governors, and this is *the* political problem."[1] And thought must be given to generating a satisfactory (let us not flinch from the phrase) governing class. That there must be such a class is, I think, beyond peradventure.

Andrew Jackson, the original populist, said any American could fill any office. Lenin, expressing himself with uncharacteristic concision, said, "Any cook can run the state." The most recent populist who tried to run the United States (Jimmy Carter) learned to his sorrow that Washington politics is a complex profession—a vocation, not an avocation. He was dealing in Congress with professionals, many of whom were there before he came to town, and who planned to be there long after he left. The day of the "citizen legislator"—the day when a legislator's primary job was something other than government—is gone. A great state cannot be run by "citizen legislators" and amateur administrators.

However, I tremble for my country when I think that schools may be sending forth into government people who are too proudly "practical" to take ideas seriously. Although, God (like His servant Senator Pat Moynihan) knows, such "practical" people have government pretty much to themselves these days. Moynihan writes:

> I have served in the Cabinet or sub-Cabinet of four Presidents. I do not believe I have ever heard at a Cabinet meeting a serious discussion of political ideas—one concerned with how men, rather than markets, behave. These are the necessary first questions of government. The Constitution of the United States is an immensely intricate

judgment as to how men will behave, given the circumstances of the time in which it was written. It is not at all clear that it is working well, given the circumstances of the present age. But this is never discussed.[2]

Actually, there is only one "first question" of government, and it is "How should we live?" or (this is the same question) "What kind of people do we want our citizens to be?" But Moynihan's basic point is bang on: Statesmen who are unaware of the ideas that shaped the institutions currently in their custody, and uninterested in the ideas that shape the expectations and tolerances of the citizenry, are statesmen governed by forces they cannot comprehend. Such statesmen are apt to think they have more range for effective action than they actually have. And they are apt to have less than they would have were they more aware of the connections between the life of the mind and the life of society.

"There is the world of ideas and the world of practice," wrote Matthew Arnold. A university can be a world of ideas (although Montaigne in his tower room is not the model emulated by many professors). And there are spheres of society that can be spheres of practice, purely. But government should not be one of them. What I have seen in a dozen years in Washington, a proudly "practical" city, has strengthened my conviction that ideas have consequences, and that the contemplation of ideas is an intensely practical undertaking.

Government is, increasingly and necessarily, conducted by specialists. Progress requires specialization. But specialization entails neglect of many necessary things. That endangers progress and, ultimately, civilization. An awareness is necessary of the intellectual soil in which today's practices and problems grew.

The United States had a founding moment, presided over by articulate Founding Fathers. They produced one founding document (the Declaration of Independence) that is a highly charged declaration of a political philosophy, and another document (the Constitution) whose interpretation has shaped every phase of American history and has produced, in Supreme Court rulings and dissents, a body of public philosophy. So it is mistaken to say that America has got along nicely without political philosophizing. The nation has produced few great treatises on political philosophy, but that is, in part, because this nation, more than any other, is a work of political philosophy. However, if institutions are to maintain the pulse of life, they must be animated by constant recurrence to a justifying doctrine. My argument is that some thinkers long dead have defined the tasks of today's government, and their definition is inadequate and, in the long run, dangerous.

Political philosophy is a quest for coherent principles of social experience. But it also often is, and is in my case, a blend of complaint and prophecy—complaint about the course of events and prophecy of worse to come unless the philosopher is heeded. I shall not disguise, or delay deploying, the implication of my argument. It is that liberal democratic societies are ill founded. If true, this is an especially melancholy bulletin for the most thoroughly liberal democratic nation, the United States, Aristotle said about reasoning that a little mistake at the beginning becomes a big mistake at the end. In politics, a big mistake at the founding can bring on the end of what was founded.

The greatest moment of American rhetoric culminated in the resolve that this Republic "shall not perish from the earth." I am not predicting that it will soon perish, but I am saying that we are systematically (that is, as a result of a philosophic system) ignoring advice Abraham Lincoln gave four years before his adjuration at Gettysburg. In 1859 he said:

> It is said an Eastern monarch once charged his wise men to invent him a sentence, to be ever in view, and which should be true and appropriate in all times and situations.

They presented him the words: "And this, too, shall pass away."[3]

But, Lincoln continued, let us hope that that is not quite true, and that we may endure by "the best cultivation of the physical world, beneath and around us; and the intellectual and moral world within us."[4]

Through two centuries of cultivating the physical world, Americans have been prodigies of productivity. But for two centuries some persons—often conservatives, like De Tocqueville and Henry Adams—have worried that this preoccupation with the physical world, and with commerce, has meant reckless neglect of the "moral world." This is a *political* worry, because it concerns fitness for republican government. "Perhaps the only moral trust with any certainty in our hands," said Edmund Burke, "is the care of our own time."[5] By inadequate fulfillment of that trust we are risking what Burke called "the most important of all revolutions," a "revolution in sentiments, manners and moral opinions."[6]

It will be said, instantly and energetically and broadly, that "sentiments, manners and moral opinions" are none of the government's business. Are they not "private" and properly beyond the legitimate concern of public agencies? No, they are not.

Keats said the world is a "vale of soul-making." I say statecraft is soulcraft. Just as all education is moral education because learning conditions conduct, much legislation is moral legislation because it conditions the action and the thought of the nation in broad and important spheres in life.

It is generally considered obvious that government should not, indeed cannot legislate morality. But in fact it does so, frequently; it should do so more often; and it never does anything more important. By the legislation of morality I mean the enactment of laws and implementation of policies that proscribe, mandate, regulate, or subsidize behavior that will, over time, have the predictable effect of nurturing, bolstering or altering habits, dispositions and values on a broad scale.

Ever since the church replaced the city as the custodian of virtue, the political order has been at best ambivalent about the need to be concerned about the inner lives of the people. The modern political order, hyperactive as it is, must of necessity have large consequence on the character of its citizenry. And it is, among other things, untidy and aesthetically displeasing for government to deny that it does what it cannot avoid doing. Government would do better what it does if it would admit what it is doing. The aim of government is justice, which is more apt to come about if government is more aware of, and forthright about, the fact that statecraft is, inevitably, soulcraft. Therefore it is odd, though explicable, that so many intelligent people say government cannot or should not do what, in fact, it does in manifest and manifold ways.

In a famous opinion in a famous case (one concerning compulsory flag salutes in schools), Justice Felix Frankfurter wrote:

> Law is concerned with external behavior and not with the inner life of man.[6]

I am not sure what Frankfurter meant. I am sure that what he said cannot be true. The purpose of this book is to say why that proposition is radically wrong.

Having said that, I can sense the "clicks" of minds closing. Most Americans probably consider Frankfurter's statement not just true, but a truism. But it was not true of American law when Felix Frankfurter was teaching and construing the law. It has never been true of American government. The idea that governments should be neutral in major conflicts about social values is only slightly more peculiar than the idea that governments can be neutral. It is important to understand not just why Frankfurter was wrong, but why a man that wise could be so wrong.

It has been said that few things can be as embarrassing as learning the pedigree of one's ideas. Frankfurter's idea has a long and distinguished pedigree that includes names important to the founding of this Republic: Locke, Jefferson, Madison. Their thoughts help explain the great paradox of modern politics: As government has become omnipresent and omniprovident regarding material well-being, the jurisdiction of politics has contracted and the dignity of the political vocation has withered.

But a philosophic tradition that supports a different conclusion than Frankfurter reached about law and "the inner life of man" has a longer and, I believe, more distinguished pedigree. This book is, in part, an exercise in intellectual archeology; its aim is to bring that tradition back to light, and to life. It is said that Paul Valéry, meeting Albert Einstein, asked: "Master, what do you do to keep track of all these ideas you keep generating?" Einstein replied: "But I've had only two ideas in my whole life." Even allowing for the fact that Einstein evidently had exacting standards concerning what counts as a new idea, it is fun to think that you have generated only two fewer than he did. But dusting off old ideas, not generating new ones, is my aim. Whatever else may be fairly said of the ideas advanced here, they will not, I hope, be stigmatized as novel. Indeed, my main point is that they involve a core consensus of the Western political tradition as first defined by Aristotle, and as added to by Burke and others. The ideas are not even new in the American political context. If they seem so, that is because they have been only hesitantly and sporadically advocated here, and because Americans have moved—sometimes marching self-consciously, sometimes wandering absentmindedly— away from propositions which in other places and other times have been considered common sense.

My thesis is that the most important task confronting Americans as a polity is, in part, a philosopher's task. The task is to reclaim for politics a properly great and stately jurisdiction. It is to rescue politics from the stale, false notion that government is always and only an instrument of coercion, making disagreeable (even when necessary) excisions from freedom, which is understood as Hobbes understood it, as "the silence of the law." It may seem strange to hear such a notion from someone who counts himself in the conservative tradition. But today the values of that tradition are threatened less by "big" government than by an abdication by the government. There is a withering away of the state regarding concern for the intangible prerequisites of free government.

For several centuries there has been abroad in the world a social romanticism, according to which almost all institutions almost always suffocate the natural virtue of the individual. Nowadays, many people inclined to think that way count themselves liberals, and yet are not reluctant to expand the size and number of the institutions of the state. Conservatives, on the other hand, are temperamentally inclined to worry about the insufficiency of virtue. Yet their visceral hostility toward government causes them to agree with liberals that governmental institutions should strive to be indifferent to, or neutral about, the "inner life"—the character—of the citizenry.

There is a tension between the belief still professed by contemporary liberalism in the natural, spontaneous flowering of the individual's spirit and the statism of the liberal program for material amelioration. However, there is a comparable tension within contemporary conservatism. Conservatives worry in collective categories and govern in terms of severe individualism. They are anxious about the moral makeup of "society," yet believe that the public interest is produced by the spontaneous cooperation of individuals making arrangements in free markets. And this is often not an empirical conclusion, but a philosophic premise. The conservative's point is not just that the public interest is usually best served by private arrangements; the point is that the public interest is necessarily produced that way. The social good is, by definition, the aggregate of whatever effects individuals produce through voluntary arrangements.

In the argument between contemporary liberals and conservatives there is a good deal less than meets—than assaults—the ear. My argument with both liberals and conservatives is about how political argument ought to proceed. My aim is to inoculate contemporary political controversy with a kind of complexity I find lacking. My thesis has this perhaps entertaining implication: Just as the nation is said to be saturated with "conservatism," I am arguing that there are almost no conservatives, properly understood.

Common sense, reason and history all teach that "strong government conservatism" is not a contradiction in terms. My support for popular sovereignty stops short of passively accepting the common usage of the word "conservative" that obscures—indeed, turns inside out—the real nature of conservatism. I will do many things for my country, but I will not pretend that the careers of, say, Ronald Reagan and Franklin Roosevelt involve serious philosophical differences. Reagan's fierce and ideological liberalism of the Manchester school and F.D.R.'s mild and improvised social-democratic program are both honorable persuasions. But they should not march under borrowed banners. They are versions of the basic program of the liberal-democratic political impulse that was born with Machiavelli and Hobbes. Near the core of the philosophy of modern liberalism, as it descends from those two men, is an inadequacy that is becoming glaring. And what in America is called conservatism is only marginally disharmonious with liberalism. This kind of conservatism is an impotent critic of liberalism because it too is a participant in the modern political enterprise, which is the subject of the next chapter. That enterprise is a radical revision of the political objectives of ancient and medieval political philosophers. The enterprise is not wrong because it revises, or even because it revises radically. Rather, it is wrong because it lowers, radically. It deflates politics, conforming politics to the strongest and commonest impulses in the mass of men.

Aristotle was the first consciously conservative philosopher because of his premise that what *is* generally predominates over what ought to be. But he is a founder of conservatism, properly understood, because his realism did not preclude a politics that takes its bearings from what ought to be. The United States acutely needs a real conservatism, characterized by a concern to cultivate the best persons and the best in persons. It should express renewed appreciation for the ennobling functions of government. It should challenge the liberal doctrine that regarding one important dimension of life—the "inner life"—there should be less government—less than there is now, less than there recently was, less than most political philosophers have thought prudent.

Political philosophy is about "the polity," which is much more than governmental institutions. It includes all the institutions, dispositions, habits and mores on which government depends and on which, therefore, government should strive to have a shaping influence. No country is "a thing of mere physical locality." A hotel is a physical locality; hotels have residents. Countries do not have residents: they have citizens. Democratic government must be a tutor as well as a servant to its citizens, because citizenship is a state of mind.

CHAPTER TWO

The Defect

> *This policy of supplying by opposite and ri-*
> *val interests, the defect of better motives ...*
> —JAMES MADISON

IN THE FIRST century before the birth of Christ, a lawyer in Rome said that "high-mindedness, magnanimity, courtesy, justice and generosity are much more in accordance with nature than pleasure, riches or even life itself."[1] In the eighteenth century after the birth of Christ (or, perhaps more to the point, exactly two centuries after the birth of Thomas Hobbes), a lawyer in Virginia said: "Those who know mankind, black as it is, must know that mankind are . . . attached to their interest."[2]

Well, now. Strong-minded fellows like Cicero and John Marshall cannot be expected to agree about everything. But their stark disagreement about fundamental things is portentous. One expects a bit of change over the course of two millennia, but the change exemplified by these two statesmen is not only especially striking; it is the defining fact of politics as we practice it.

At issue are two ostensibly empirical propositions by two reflective statesmen. At stake are two understandings of the

25

purpose of politics. One proposition, Cicero's or Marshall's, is bound to be truer than the other, but it is notoriously difficult to determine the truth of such propositions. So the question for statesmen is not so much which proposition is "true" as it is which understanding of the political task is more prudent. Cicero's proposition may seem less plausible than Marshall's as a description of everyday experience, but it is more prudent as an animating principle of politics. The problem for modern persons considering Cicero's proposition is the idea of nature. That is the heart of the matter, and I shall approach it through two things close to my heart.

Baseball (to put first things first) and politics are two activities about which I spend a lot of my life thinking. Naturally ("the natural" is a concept to which I shall recur), I have a strong desire to justify this investment of time. If you accept the premise of our political system, you accept the fact that it is natural that my reason should serve my desire by devising a rationalization for my preoccupation with baseball and politics. So I begin this book with a confession of self-interestedness (another subject to which I shall recur). According to some cynics who masquerade as philosophers, and some philosophers whose philosophy conduces to cynicism, philosophy is generally a rationalization of desires. I disagree, but I admit that my aim is to explain why politics and baseball are more noble undertakings than is today generally understood. Asserting the nobility of baseball may seem merely peculiar, but asserting the nobility of the political vocation may seem perverse. To understand a reassertion of the grandeur of politics, you must risk a crick in your neck. You must look back over your shoulder at the long sweep of political philosophy, since it was invented by Plato.

The Greeks believed that sports were a religious and civic—in a word, moral—undertaking. They are morally serious because man's noblest aim is loving contemplation of worthy things, such as beauty. By using our bodies beautifully we teach the soul to understand and love it. A purpose of politics is to facilitate, as much as is prudent, the existence of worthy passions and the achievement of worthy aims. It is to help persons want what they ought to want. Politics should share one purpose with religion: the steady emancipation of the individual through the education of his passions.

The essence of the ancients' philosophy was this proposition: Man is naturally social, so his happiness is contingent upon the congruence of his society and his nature. The greatest modern political philosopher to take the ancients' view of things was Burke. He was a man of Ciceronean (and Lincolnesque) rhetorical gifts. This is not coincidental: If you believe in the better angels of our nature, and that the purpose of politics is to summon them, you shall do so with rhetoric. Burke believed, as Cicero did, that human beings "are bound, and are generally disposed, to look up with reverence to the best patterns of the species."[3] He said the best patterns are from "a 'natural' aristocracy, without which there is no nation," and added:

> The state of civil society which necessarily generates this aristocracy is a state of Nature—and much more truly so than a savage and incoherent mode of life. For man is by nature reasonable, and he is never perfectly in his natural state but when he is placed where reason may be best cultivated and most predominates.[4]

Because a well-ordered polity is a prerequisite for such excellence, the political vocation is good and the estate of government is grand:

> . . . the state ought not to be considered as nothing better than a partnership agreement in a trade of pepper and coffee, calico, or tobacco, or some such low concern. . . . It is to be looked upon with other reverence, because it is not a partnership in things subservient only to the gross

animal existence of a temporary and perishable nature. It
is a partnership in all science; a partnership in all art; a
partnership in every virtue and in all perfection. As the
ends of such a partnership cannot be obtained in many
generations, it becomes a partnership not only between
those who are living, but between those who are living,
those who are dead, and those who are to be born.[5]

Which is more amusing, the number of Marxists who have
never cracked a volume of *Das Kapital,* or the number of today's *soi-disant* conservatives who have been so busy praising
Burke they have not taken time to read, or at least comprehend,
him? It is perhaps marvelous that people who preach disdain
for government can consider themselves the intellectual descendants of Burke, the author of a celebration of the state.
But surely it is peculiar—worse, it is larcenous—for people to
expropriate the name "conservative" while remaining utterly
unsympathetic to the central tenet of the greatest modern conservative.

Burke's thought was a gloriously bright but isolated flaring
of a vanishing tradition. The future belonged to the intellectual
descendants of another Englishman, Thomas Hobbes. It was
Hobbes whose thought fitted the future of Burke's country,
and fitted even better the republic that Burke's rhetoric sup-
ported in rebellion against Burke's country.

Of course, Hobbes had a predecessor. The political philosophy of modernity began (we may say for convenience) in a
thin essay by a thin Florentine whose maxims for the guidance
of the maneuvering princes of Italian city-states helped bring
on the world in which we live, a permanent social revolution
fueled by economic dynamism. In the American republic, as in
Machiavelli's political universe, the fundamental fact is restless
energy. The quest of classical political philosophy was for a
polity at a still point of virtuous equilibrium. Machiavelli's
quest was for rules that would enable men to ride and direct

the whirlwind of endless social dynamism. This founding father of modern politics was preoccupied with the distinction between those contingencies which are, and those which are not, subject to control by political skill. Until Machiavelli, the task of political philosophy was to solve man's fundamental problem, which was to answer the question "How ought I to live?" With Machiavelli, political philosophy became concerned with solving the politician's problem, which was understood to be keeping order and keeping power. What made Machiavelli so indicative of a new age is less what he said than his saying of it. Worldly people were not amazed by his idea that civil and moral life may depend on political practices that are uncivil and immoral. What was remarkable was that the world had reached a point where such things were said in a matter-of-fact tone of voice. Machiavelli was subversive of beliefs and practices, but especially of pretenses.

However, even more than Machiavelli, Hobbes was the bridge between the ancients and the moderns. He was so because of his radicalism, which was the result of his philosophic depth and logical clarity. It is said that Hobbes, in middle age, chanced upon an open book of geometry and experienced an epiphany which left him indelibly marked. If so, it was an intellectual's mid-life crisis that helped change the world.

Although Hobbes believed that the conduct of politics should be shaped with reference to nature, it is a different facet of nature to which he referred. Hitherto, political philosophy had held that the "state of nature," meaning the natural state for man, was in a well-ordered society. (As Burke put it, the "state of civil society . . . where reason may be best cultivated and most predominates."[6]) But Hobbes held that the state of nature was prior to civil society, and severely defective. However, the defects, he maintained, could be corrected by a cleverly constructed civil society. Henceforth political philosophy took its bearing not from the ends men ought to seek and which a few can approach, but rather from the beginnings that all men share —from the strongest, most elemental desires and passions. Liberalism came quickly to the "social contract" metaphor, because it locates the origins of government in an agreement between rational, self-interested but pre-civic persons. They are motivated to associate neither by neighborliness (affection) nor political allegiance (shared public philosophy) but only by anxiety about their physical safety and the security of their property.

Long before Einstein told us that matter is energy, Machiavelli and Hobbes and other modern political philosophers defined man as a lump of matter whose most politically relevant attribute is a form of energy called "self-interestedness." This was not a portrait of man "warts and all." It was all wart— except that the dominating attribute was not considered a blemish. The analysis was not judgmental. The portrait of man as concentrated self-interestedness scanted other attributes. But by treating as negligible the political relevance of other attributes, such as cultural, ethnic and class particularities, modern political philosophy achieved the conception it needed of man as political animal. This was a conception without attributes that could complicate—with too many variables—the equation involved in solving the problem of social control. That was the problem which intrigued Hobbes, who found the decay of Tudor political arrangements as intellectually stimulating as Machiavelli found the (Hobbesian) chaos prevailing among rival Italian princes.

If you believe in natural law, in norms apprehensible by common judgment, you are apt to believe that the capacity of individuals to reach judgments is a source of social cohesion: individuals are apt to concur in some important judgments. However, if you do not believe in natural law, you are apt to believe that the individual capacity for private judgment is a problem, that social discord is its probable consequence. And no amount of insistence on the existence of "self-evident" truths can paper over the problem. Hobbes met it squarely, with a bold philosophy of mind that made him and his intellectual descendant John Locke the intellectual co-founders of the liberal democratic state. Although Hobbes expressed it with characteristic bluntness and Locke with characteristic indirection, they both began from the premise that the mainspring of human action is calculation, and that the calculation is controlled by strong passions, including fear of violent death and desire for self-preservation.

Why is military conscription such a difficult issue for liberal democratic states? Because the means necessary to protect such states often conflict with the reasons for such states. The issue of conscription brings into high relief the general and perennial dilemma of liberal democratic societies: How do you promote the general, corporate interest in societies founded with explicit and exclusive reference to individual self-interestedness? The solution (if it can be so called) to this problem is a "realistic" redefinition of the public interest. Because individuals are self-interested, the public interest must be connected as closely as possible with the achievement of private interests. The connection is achieved by semantic fiat, by defining the public good as the aggregate of results of the free pursuit of private interests. This connection has costs, intellectual and moral and social. The moral and social costs, to which I shall come, are, I think, still mounting. The intellectual cost is the damage done to the idea that a liberal democratic society takes more seriously than any other: the idea of freedom.

Freedom, said Kant, is "autonomy," meaning "the property of the will to be a law to itself."[7] But that idea of autonomy was rendered dubious by the philosophic doctrines of the intellectual founders of the liberal democratic orders. Man, they said, is free by virtue of possessing reason, but reason is enslaved to natural passions which man does not choose. Reason without passion is science; even—in theory—political science. But the premise of modern politics is reason in the service of passion. Hobbes, the epistemologist-as-politician, said that "the Thoughts are to the Desires, as Scouts, and Spies, to range abroad, and find the way to the Things Desired."[8] A century later, David Hume (who died in 1776, the birth date of the first modern nation) sounded the same theme: "Reason is, and only ought to be the slave of the passions, and can never pretend to any other office than to serve and obey them."[9] If so, what elevates man above other creatures is not a nobler end, but a more effective means (reason) of doing as animals do: following appetites.

Popular sovereignty may give people mastery over their government, but the celebration must be muted if, as Jeremy Bentham said, "Nature has placed mankind under the governance of two sovereign masters, *pain* and *pleasure*. It is for them alone to point out what we ought to do, as well as to determine what we shall do. . . . They govern us in all we do. . . . In words a man may pretend to abjure their empire: but in reality he will remain subject to it all the while."[10] The sovereign populace may be master of the government, but the populace is composed of individuals who do not govern themselves. However, the good news of modernity is that passion at least regulates other passions: Fear renders men willing to accept limits on their aggressiveness and acquisitiveness. Reason is subservient to the passions, but the passions are to be held in check. They are to be limited not by standards of virtue but only by the requirements of commodious living among other passionate people. Or to put the point slightly differently, the scope of the passions is to be circumscribed only by the virtue of tolerance. That becomes the foremost (and perhaps the only) public virtue in a society composed of people endowed with equal rights grounded in their common passions.

The only value almost as esteemed as tolerance in a liberal

democratic society is directly related to tolerance. It is compassion, which involves, in practice, the essence of Lockean politics: preoccupation with the material and commonplace human needs. The duty to be tolerant derives from an egalitarian definition of rights rooted in the passions, and especially the passion for "well-being." The modern idea is that political rights accrue to human beings simply by virtue of their humanness, not by virtue of any qualities less universal. Instead of encouraging mankind to have a passion for virtue, modernity makes a political virtue of the most prosaic passions. The virtue (meaning utility) of the passions derives from their universality, regularity and strength. These are attributes essential to the new science of politics.

Self-interest, says De Tocqueville, is "the only immutable point in the human heart."[11] Its immutability, far from being cause for sorrow, is, to the modern mind, its beauty. The immutability is what recommends it as a foundation for the political order. Sir William Blackstone, whose *Commentaries* did so much to shape the legal profession in the early years of this republic of lawyers, wrote: "The only true and natural foundations of society are the wants and fears of individuals."[12] By "true" I take him to have meant "efficacious." In the mass of men, said the greatest American jurist (Marshall), "judgment is completely controlled by the passions."[13] What, then, of the famous statement by the most revered American jurist, Oliver Wendell Holmes, that "the best test of truth is the power of the thought to get accepted in the competition of the market"?[14] Markets test popularity, not truth. Holmes called "the power of the thought to get accepted" the "best" test of truth not because it was good, but because he believed there was no better one. No wonder. He believed what modern political philosophy has taught: Society is just a marketplace officiated by government; and an "idea" is either a passion or a product of reason, which is a "spy" for passion. Thus the epistemology of modern liberalism can lead to deep irrationalism, such as Holmes's, and to the irrationality of First Amendment law as it has evolved in the direction set by his dissents.

When Hume says that in the founding of a regime, "every man must be supposed a knave,"[15] the highly charged word "knave" means only "a self-interested creature." There is an incongruity: The word is judgmental; the phenomenon is natural. The term deplores, yet denotes something as steady and inevitable as the law of gravity, as certain as a law of geometry. "I shall consider human actions and appetites," said Benedict Spinoza, "just as if it were a question of lines, planes and solids."[16] If the science of government is the geometry of motion, governments should run like fine machinery. "Governments, like clocks," said William Penn, "go from the motion men give them." Well, then, society should resemble one of the games that amused eighteenth-century intellectuals—billiards, with its pleasing precision of angles and controlled caroms, one ball imparting motion to another. Or perhaps chess. "In the great chess board of human society," wrote Adam Smith (the author of what Jefferson called "the best book extant on political economy"), "every single piece has a principle of motion of its own altogether different from that which the legislature might choose to impress upon it."[17] It would be folly for the legislature to want to impress its own principle of motion on persons, because to do so would disrupt the useful regularity of human behavior.

Smith said the magic word of modernity: "society." Once it was thought that history was driven by God's will. But the eighteenth century took to heart the thought that the very structure of society is history's engine. In the nineteenth century, reacting against the eighteenth century's celebration of society's autonomy, and excited by the example of Napoleon, some thinkers eagerly insisted on the history-making role of exceptional individuals. But the eighteenth century had internalized the idea that society is an arena where self-interested individuals are unintentionally united in unconscious obedience to general laws and the unwitting production of the public good. This theory drained from the study of history much of the element of personal drama; but as compensation, it nourished the illusion that history is orderly and progressive.

Eighteenth-century philosophers, who were fascinated by astronomy, noticed that the beneficent order of the universe is not the result of stars and suns' intending the general good of the universe. And the philosophers came to a similar conclusion about society: A good society is remarkably independent of individuals' willing the social good. A good society is a lumpy stew of individuals and groups, each with its own inherent "principle of motion." This stew stirs itself, and in the fullness of time, out comes a creamy pureé called "the public interest." This is the Cuisinart theory of justice. The endless maelstrom of individuals' pursuing private goods produces, magically, the public good. But of course it is not done by magic at all; it is done by definition.

The elevation of society in mankind's esteem meant the demotion of politics and government. "Society," said Thomas Paine, "is produced by our wants and government by our wickedness." Because "society performs for itself almost every thing which is ascribed to government." Government must merely "supply the few cases to which society and civilization are not conveniently competent."[18] If society is understood as an arena for the exercise of the passions, government is degraded by being justified only in terms of a low—albeit necessary—assignment: policing the arena to limit anarchy. Bentham believed (and a great many who today call themselves conservatives believe) that government is simply coercive, that "the whole of government is but a connected series of . . . sacrifices." Therefore, Bentham said: "It is to the interest of the public that the portion of respect which, along with the salary, is habitually at-

tached to any office should be as small as possible."[19] That sour
sentiment, shared by a nineteenth-century philosophic radical
and twentieth-century "conservatives," brings me to modernity's destination: America.

On May 12, 1780, with the Republic struggling to be born
through war, John Adams wrote to Abigail from Paris:

> To take a Walk in the Gardens of the Palace of the
> Tuilleries, and describe the Statues there, all in marble, in
> which the ancient Divinities and Heroes are represented
> with exquisite Art, would be a very pleasant Amusement,
> and instructive Entertainment, improving in History,
> Mythology, Poetry, as well as in Statuary. Another Walk
> in the Gardens of Versailles, would be usefull and agre-
> able. But to observe these Objects with Taste and de-
> scribe them so as to be understood, would require more
> time and thought than I can possibly Spare. It is not indeed
> the fine Arts, which our Country requires. The Usefull,
> the mechanic Arts, are those which We have occasion for
> in a young Country, as yet simple and not far advanced in
> Luxury, altho perhaps much too far for her Age and
> Character.
>
> I could fill volumes with Descriptions of Temples and
> Palaces, Paintings, Sculptures, Tapestry, Porcelaine, &c, &c,
> &c,—if I could have time. But I could not do this without
> neglecting my duty.—The Science of Government it is my
> Duty to Study, more than all other Sciences: the Art of
> Legislation and Administration and Negotiation, ought to
> take Place, indeed to exclude in a manner all other Arts.—I
> must study Politicks and War that my sons may have lib-
> erty to study Mathematicks and Philosophy. My sons
> ought to study Mathematicks and Philosophy, Geography,
> natural History, Naval Architecture, navigation, Com-
> merce and Agriculture, in order to give their Children a
> right to study Painting, Poetry, Musick, Architecture,
> Statuary, Tapestry and Porcelaine.[20]

That is the voice of a civilized modern man, a man with an appreciation of fine things, but feeling only resignation and resentment toward politics as a necessary duty that distracts him from fine things. Adams makes the public-spirited modern man's best case for politics: It is not good, but it makes many good things possible. Politics constitutes the basic level of a three-part edifice: The political order is a foundation facilitating the production of wealth, which in turn facilitates the flowering of culture. Or, as Hobbes said, "*Leisure* is the mother of *philosophy;* and *Commonwealth* the mother of *peace* and *leisure.*"[21]

So we hope. However, the spirit of modern politics is not hopefulness but wariness. The experiences of the twentieth century (Hitler, Stalin, Mao) have understandably deepened the tendency to think that the ancients organized political reflection around the wrong question. They asked: "Who is most eligible to rule?" Perhaps the right question is: "How do we prevent the worst from happening?" Perhaps the Founding Fathers were uncannily prescient. Their political philosophy involves a negative catechism:

> *What is the worst that can happen, politically?*
> Tyranny.
> *To what form of tyranny is popular government prey?*
> A tyrannical majority.
> *How can that be prevented?*
> By the checks and balances of a system of separation of powers, and federalism, in government; and by having a large, complex commercial society that will spawn a "saving multiplicity of factions," and will submerge dangerous passions in the pursuit of gain.

In the most famous of *The Federalist Papers*, Madison says: "In the extent and proper structure of the Union . . . we behold a Republican remedy for the diseases most incident to

Republican Government."[22] The "proper structure" involves the checks and balances of the separation of powers, and the dispersal of powers through a federal system. All this is designed to channel and manipulate self-interestedness into a social equilibrium. ("Ambition must be made to counteract ambition. The interest of the man must be connected with the constitutional rights of the place."[23]) That is, public-spiritedness will not be assumed, or even necessary, even in public officials. The "extent" of the Union refers to the question of scale, the special suitability of an "extensive republic" for popular government. Democracies fail when they do not have an adequate "number of citizens and extent of territory."

> The smaller the society, the fewer probably will be the distinct parties and interests composing it; the fewer the distinct parties and interests, the more frequently will a majority be found of the same party; and the smaller the number of individuals composing a majority, and the smaller the compass within which they are placed, the more easily will they concert and execute their plans of oppression. Extend the sphere, and you take in a greater variety of parties and interests; you make it less probable that a majority of the whole will have a common motive to invade the rights of other citizens; or if such a common motive exists, it will be more difficult for all who feel it to discover their own strength, and to act in unison with each other.[24]

This is the Madisonian revolution in democratic theory. Hitherto, philosophers had agreed that if democracy was feasible at all, it would be feasible only in a small, face-to-face society, like Pericles' Athens or Rousseau's Geneva. This was thought to be so because factions were thought to be the bane of democracy. The smaller the society, the more one could hope for homogeneity. Madison stood this idea on its head,

arguing for a "saving multiplicity of factions." To that end,
Madison made a sociologically subtle amendment to Locke's
proposition that "the great and chief end . . . of men's uniting
into commonwealths and putting themselves under government
is the preservation of their property."[25] Madison wrote that
"the most common and durable source of factions, has been the
various and unequal distribution of property."[26] He was asserting the usefulness not only of differences in the amounts
but also in the kinds of property owned (and hence the kinds
of "interests" generated). It is kinds of property that are con-
noted by the word "different" in Madison's famous proposition that "the first object of government" is "protection of
different and unequal faculties of acquiring property."[27]

Madison further wrote: "Either the existence of the same
passion or interest in a majority at the same time, must be pre-
vented; or the majority, having such a co-existent passion or interest, must be rendered, by their number and local situation,
unable to concert and carry into effect schemes of oppression."[28] Madison's "either/or" formulation suggests that the
two alternatives are exhaustive, but not exclusive. There must
be a plenitude of passions among the multiplicity of factions to
prevent the existence of a stable and tyrannical majority; and
there must be the auxiliary precaution of institutional inhibitions on the fulfillment of the passion of such a majority,
should it materialize. Madison's attention is exclusively on
controlling passions with countervailing passions; he is not
concerned with the amelioration or reform of passions. The
political problem is seen entirely in terms of controlling the
passions that nature gives, not nurturing the kind of character
that the polity might need. He says, "We well know that
neither moral nor religious motives can be relied on."[29]

The development of mass media and other features of a national culture has not nationalized opinion; it has not obliter-

ated regional differences and local preoccupations; it has not raised unmanageable waves of opinion or dangerous uniformity. Furthermore, were Madison to return today, he probably would be most surprised—and chagrined—by the susceptibility of the American political system to paralysis at the hands of the multiplicity of factions. The multiplicity may help save us from an overbearing majority, but it may expose us to governmental gridlock. Nevertheless, Madison was correct about the danger of tyrannical majorities. The precautions established by the framers of the Constitution and the authors of the first ten amendments have sufficed to keep that danger manageable. This sufficiency results, in part, from the social diversity of this continental nation. It results, in part, also from the largely unanticipated but by-and-large salutary role of judicial review in restraining majoritarianism.

But prudent political thinkers have more worries than appear prominently in Madison's philosophy. The American Founders talked almost exclusively about institutional arrangements and the sociology of the factions presupposed by the institutional arrangements. They talked little about the sociology of virtue, or the husbandry of exemplary elites—the "best patterns of the species" of which Burke wrote. Perhaps this is because they assumed that the necessity of constant, systematic concern for the cultivation of character was plain as a pikestaff; perhaps it is because the continuous existence in America of an aristocracy of public-spirited talents was assumed. Rashly.

It has been said that Madison Avenue is, symbolically, the Main Street of Madison's republic. Certainly the advertising industry strives to be a pyromaniac igniting conflagrations of appetites in that unfailingly dry tinder, the American consumer. Hume spoke of "envy, the spur to industry." To the extent that advertising involves the steady inculcation of envy and other forms of restlessness and psychic motion (I know advertising is more complicated and useful than that), it is part of society's fuel.

However that may be, there is a striking disproportion between Madison's importance in the shaping of the nation, and the nation's memorials to him. The nation's capital is named after the wrong Founding Father. It should be the city of Madison. The fact that the only public building in Washington named for Madison is an annex to the Library of Congress suggests how far he has faded into the recesses of the nation's memory. A library: How low can you sink in a city where the notorious shortage of good bookstores reveals the status of thought relative to that of action? Madison has received some justice, although of the poetic sort, in Washington. One of the city's poshest hotels is The Madison. It is much favored by agents of the private sector when they come to try to bend public power to their private purposes. These are agents of factions. Look around the lobby of The Madison and you will see a rich rainbow of different and unequal capacities for acquiring property. Madison might like that. He would certainly understand.

At this point, step back and survey the intellectual context that modern political philosophy has given our world. The oldest conundrum in political philosophy is this: If there is a natural right, should not knowledge of it be natural? If because of his nature man cannot live optimally except in accordance with certain principles, why is there not agreement regarding those principles? In modernity's solution, the idea of natural law has been redefined so that it points not toward perfection but toward regularity. It does not refer to how men ought to aspire to live; it does not refer to an ideal approached by those most meriting emulation. Rather, it refers to how most men behave most of the time. Since this great redefinition, political philosophy has been grounded not on the idea of duty but on the idea of rights, and the idea of rights has been grounded in men's passional equipment. Burke wrote, disparagingly: "The little catechism of the rights of men is soon learned; and the inferences are in the passions."[30]

The fact that there have been and are such a wide variety of social catechisms causes some persons to offer a philosophic shrug, saying: Athenian ways were right for Athenians and barbarism was right for barbarians. But an irreducible question remains: Which way of living was better—meaning more in accord with the finer capacities that human beings share? The question cannot be reduced to comparison of roads or armies or GNP, or even levels of contentment. Barbarians may well wish to live barbarically. Indeed, as Aristotle said, such contentment is evidence of how degraded the barbarian condition is.

Aristotle and other ancients thought human nature contained a political compass that points toward fulfillment in a well-ordered political society. At least, the compass will point if social conditions give the compass a chance to function. Statecraft should gently pull in the direction in which the needle in human nature points.

The moderns believe that the natural vitality of human nature is a problem, involving a tension between the individual and the political order, an order that is, because of man's vitality, a regrettable necessity. It is regrettable because it is coercive; it is a limiter of "natural liberty." But modernity's stroke of genius is in the use of the problem to resolve the problem. The modern idea of liberty is grounded in necessity, in the sweep of the strongest passions. Modernity makes a virtue of necessity (and in the process makes a poor thing of the idea of virtue). Man's natural vitality, accommodated and manipulated by appropriate institutions, is to become the source of beneficent social order.

If the good is by definition pleasurable, and if the distinction between worthy and unworthy pleasures is by definition arbitrary—if pushpin really is as good as poetry—then these two definitions go far toward defining the political order. The task of restraining and transforming the appetites is replaced by the task of directing them into useful, or at least not harmful, channels. The result is a radical retrenchment, a lowering of expectations, a constriction of political horizons. By abandoning both divine and natural teleology, modernity radically reoriented politics. The focus of politics shifted away from the question of the most eligible ends of life, to the passional origins of actions. The ancients were resigned to accommodating what the moderns are eager to accommodate: human shortcomings. What once was considered a defect—self-interestedness—became the base on which an edifice of rights was erected.

Modern politics focuses on the actual rather than the potential. It enthusiastically uses the actual rather than, as the ancients did, judiciously resisting it in the name of the potential. Obviously, the actual must be accommodated. But surely the accommodation should be guided by a goal of excellence. Not so, say the moderns. Modern political philosophy has transformed a fact (man's appetitive nature) into a moral principle: Man should be allowed, even encouraged, to do what he most desires to do (consistent, of course, with other people doing likewise). The assumption is that the social good can be achieved by clever institutional arrangements which channel and manipulate the most powerful human impulses.

The abandonment of soulcraft was an abandonment of a pursuit of excellence, but it was not for that reason an act of pessimism. Rather, it was a fork in the road of optimism. Man might not be elevated, but he could be tamed. Regimes may not be elevating, but they will be perpetual. They shall be perpetual-motion machines, wonderful clockwork devices running off the natural "motion" of mankind. Once when President William Howard Taft was being briefed by a young aide who kept referring to "the machinery of government," Taft whispered to a colleague, "My God, he really thinks it's machinery." Such an idea is wrong, but not surprising.

Ancient political philosophy demanded subtle statesmanship, but held out the promise of nobility. Modern political philosophy demands less of statesmen—indeed, it insists on modest, even banal aims—but it promises clarity and certainty. The two great virtues of modern political philosophy (in its own estimation) are the related virtues of simplicity and egalitarianism. The sole publicly relevant (or publicly important) character traits—self-interestedness and tolerance—are suddenly within the reach of virtually everybody. As has been recently demonstrated in the worlds of art and academics, if you redefine excellence recklessly enough, there will be no shortage of excellence. By creative redefinition, modern political philosophy made the good social order much more accessible, and made the statesman's vocation much less exacting:

> The principle of self-interest rightly understood is not a lofty one, but it is clear and sure. It does not aim at mighty objects, but it attains without excessive exertion all those at which it aims. As it lies within the reach of all capacities, everyone can without difficulty learn and retain it. By its admirable conformity to human weaknesses it easily obtains great dominion; nor is that dominion precarious, since the principle checks one personal interest by another, and uses, to direct the passions, the very same instrument that excites them.[31]

In Plato's *Gorgias*, Pericles and other eminent Athenians are judged to have failed the first test of political leadership: the improvement of the citizens. You may think there is a becom-

ing modesty about modern political arrangements and aspirations because they depend for their success and fulfillment
upon no improvement in mankind. You may think that if nature dictates only self-interest, a society that demands more is
not only imprudent, it is unnatural. Certainly the founding
philosophers of liberal democratic societies have been anxious
to stake out the boundaries of the possible, anxious (anxiety sets
the tone of modernity) to recognize the limits to what intellect
can achieve in politics. The question is whether modernity
carries prudence to imprudent limits.

Modernity has made us free (at least to the extent that freedom really is just the absence of external restraints imposed by
others). It has made us rich (at least to the extent that a rich
life is compatible with freedom so defined, and to the extent
that we are content to measure richness in terms of the aggre-
gation of private wealth). But modernity also has made us
vulnerable. We are vulnerable because we need what modern
political philosophy discourages. Or perhaps it is better to say
we need to discourage what modern political philosophy li-
censes: disdain for politics, dislike of government and (hence)
a tenuous sense of social cohesion. Our sense of citizenship, of
social warmth and a shared fate, has become thin gruel.

Once politics is defined negatively, as an enterprise for drawing a protective circle around the individual's sphere of self-
interested action, then public concerns are by definition distinct
from, and secondary to, private concerns. Regardless of democratic forms, when people are taught by philosophy (and the
social climate) that they need not govern their actions by calculations of public good, they will come to blame all social
shortcomings on the agency of collective considerations, the
government, and will absolve themselves.

This is the dangerous logic of the modern undertaking, the
attempt to make government dependent on something less

noble and less exacting but more constant than the nurtured virtue of citizenry. A nation—a civilization—so constituted cannot long endure. It is time to reconstitute political argument.

CHAPTER THREE

Out of the Wilderness

> *It must be admitted, that civilization is oner-
> ous and expensive; hideous expense to keep
> it up;—let it go, and be Indians again; but
> why Indians?—that is costly, too; the mud-
> turtle and trout life is easier and cheaper,
> and oyster, cheaper still.*
>
> —RALPH WALDO EMERSON

THE HINGE of American history was a statement by a Senatorial candidate toward the end of the final debate in a mid-nineteenth-century campaign. He said: "We of Illinois have decided it for ourselves. We tried slavery, kept it up for twelve years, and finding that it was not profitable we abolished it for that reason."[1] With three words—"for that reason"—Stephen Douglas defined slavery as a question of price, not principle. Douglas' opponent had said of that attitude four years earlier:

> This *declared* indifference, but as I must think, covert *real* zeal for the spread of slavery, I can not but hate. . . . I hate it because it deprives our republic an example of its just influence in the world—enables the enemies of free institutions, with plausibility, to taunt us as hypocrites—causes the real friends of freedom to doubt our sincerity, and especially because it forces so many really good men amongst ourselves into an open war with the very funda-

mental principles of civil liberty—criticising the Declaration of Independence, and insisting that there is no right
principle of action but *self-interest*.[2]

The centrality of the principle of self-interest in the political
argument of a Middle Western state in the middle of the nineteenth century was, as Marxists like to say, "no accident." It
was not a peculiarity of regional political culture. Rather, it
was the result of a long, broad tradition of political reflection
that had shaped the public mind of the West from Florence,
Italy, to Peoria, Illinois.

The years in which Lincoln matured as a man and emerged
as a politician were years of struggle for the mind of the
North. The defining drama of American history, the Civil
War, was precipitated by a particular law that undertook to
teach a particular moral lesson. The law was the Kansas-
Nebraska Act. Lincoln and kindred spirits could tolerate slavery in the Deep South, convinced as they were that if confined,
slavery would be on the road to eventual extinction. But they
would wage war over the principle embodied in the Kansas-
Nebraska Act, the principle that slavery is a matter of moral
indifference, or is, at any rate, so morally trivial that the people
of Kansas and Nebraska should be free to establish or ban it as
they pleased. It was not because of an "interest," it was because
of an idea—that idea—that "the war came."

"Union forever, hurrah, boys, hurrah!" went a Civil War
song. But the boys were not fighting for the empty concept of
a "union." They were fighting—whether they understood it or
not—for a union "dedicated" to a "proposition." The Kansas-
Nebraska Act was an attempt to legislate morality. It failed. It
failed for the same reason that the most recent attempt to legislate morality—the civil rights acts of 1964 and 1965—succeeded.
It failed and they succeeded because this is still a nation "dedicated" to a "proposition."

It was with the Louisiana Purchase that Thomas Jefferson, the foremost advocate of popular sovereignty, provided the place that was to become Nebraska Territory. It was concerning that territory that Lincoln made himself the greatest American. He did so by insisting that there are limits to popular sovereignty. The crucial premise of the Declaration of Independence is that people can make a nation by making the acceptance of an idea a political act. Lincoln said: You cannot have it both ways. You cannot repeal the Missouri Compromise and retain the Declaration of Independence. Either slavery shall be forever barred from the territories, thereby placing it on a path to certain eventual extinction, or the nation can no longer pretend to rest on the bedrock principle that "all men are created equal." Lincoln's point was that fidelity to the Declaration requires placing some questions beyond the reach of majorities, and thus placing some values above popular sovereignty.

Early in that final, seventh debate, Douglas had said:

> Our fathers knew when they made the government, that the laws and institutions which were well adapted to the green mountains of Vermont, were unsuited to the rice plantations of South Carolina. They knew then, as well as we know now, that the laws and institutions which would be well adapted to the beautiful prairies of Illinois would not be suited to the mining regions of California. They knew that in a Republic as broad as this, having such a variety of soil, climate and interest, there must necessarily be a corresponding variety of local laws—the policy and institutions of each State adapted to its condition and wants. For this reason this Union was established on the right of each State to do as it pleased on the question of slavery, and every other question.[3]

In the modern manner, Douglas reduced politics to material and economic factors. His political vocabulary dealt with concrete, tangible things: mountains, prairies, soil, climate, rice, mining. Madison wanted an "extensive" Republic, and by Douglas' day the republic was indeed "broad." And Douglas spoke the language of Madisonianism, the language of "interest," or—what is the same thing—"wants." His rhetoric radiated the assumption that any question, even slavery, can be reduced to material and economic considerations, and hence every question can be decided through popular sovereignty, which exists to express "wants." All political questions can be decided the same way because all political questions are about "wants," and all "wants" are equally eligible.

But Lincoln believed that there can be closed questions in an open society. Indeed, a society that has no closed questions cannot count on remaining an open society. Citizenship is a state of mind. A completely and permanently open mind will be an empty mind—if it is a mind at all. A mind cannot be shapeless; it must be moulded. And "he who moulds public sentiment goes deeper than he who enacts statutes and pronounces decisions. He makes statutes and decisions possible or impossible to be executed."[4] He who moulds public opinion makes or breaks the nation, because "A nation may be said to consist of its territory, its people, and its laws. The territory is the only part which is certain of durability."[5]

Government that rests on convention and other forms of opinion can be transformed by transformations of opinion. If government is to be more than "responsive" to social forces, if it is to shape and lead those forces, including tides of opinion, it must be concerned with the mind. It cannot trust the "self-evidence" of the polity's vital principle to ensure, automatically, the requisite adherence to those principles. The robust Jeffersonian rhetoric of self-evidence, which so shaped our understanding of the temper of our founding times, seems to express a calm confidence that today seems anachronistic. It speaks the confidence of men who felt that civilization is neither onerous nor expensive. It radiates the happy conviction that men will be civilized if only they are left free. It carries the glad tidings that men will live as men ought to live—and not as oysters, mud-turtles or trout—if only a few preconditions are supplied. The political preconditions are dramatically simple—indeed, self-evident.

The doctrine of self-evidence has affected not only how Americans treat one another but also how they feel related to the rest of the world. In his seventh message to Congress (December 2, 1823), President Monroe enunciated a doctrine: "It is impossible that the allied powers should extend their political system to any portion of either [Western Hemisphere] continent without endangering our peace and happiness; nor can anyone believe that our southern brethren, if left to themselves, would adopt it [the European system of government] of their own accord. It is equally impossible, therefore, that we should behold such interposition in any form with indifference."[6]

Monroe might have expanded his remarks as follows (had he and everyone else not considered it all self-evident): Any attempt of a European power to extend its form of government to our hemisphere would endanger our peace and happiness precisely because "our southern brethren" do not want such a government. We know they do not because said brethren are men, and we know that all men are able to apprehend their self-evident rights and (what is much the same) interests.

Among the things that are far from self-evident (in the sense of universally and immediately clear) is the meaning of the phrase "self-evident" as used by Jefferson. What it certainly does not mean is "universally and immediately clear." Its most famous use was in the opening passage of one of the most resonant polemics the world has known. The Declaration of Independence was a document of urgent practicality. The phrase "self-evident" was, in part, a flourish intended to impart momentum to a political movement, and to lend an aura of legitimacy to the desperate acts of revolution and war. The doctrine of self-evidence was, to a considerable extent, not an epistemological theory but a rhetorical mode.

But the phrase "self-evident" was, and it is, an adjectival phrase applicable to any proposition whose truth is clear to unclouded minds. Self-evident truths are clear beyond peradventure—so clear that it would be senseless to ask for evidence or grounds for them. Any mind that understands them agrees with them, and any mind can understand them if it is sufficiently purged of cant and prejudice and superstition. The second paragraph of the Declaration of Independence would have been self-evidently clear to King George III and his Prime Minister, Lord North, had their minds not been cluttered with all the bad intellectual baggage of Europe's *ancien régime*. The proposition "seven is a prime number" is a self-evident truth, although its truth is not evident to all the tribes of Micronesia. But, now, notice: To call a truth "self-evident" is not to say it is easily, let alone universally, apprehended. Such a truth can be apprehended by a certain kind of mind. And if particular "self-evident" political truths are important, then nurturing minds capable of apprehending those truths is important public business.

American experience has been the most explicit, and emphatic, break with the tradition of society shaped from "above" by central authority. From Plato through Hegel and beyond, the justification for using central authority to "moralize" society from above was that this would produce unity with harmony. But by the end of the seventeenth century, England had experienced regicide and civil war, and its disharmonies had seeded the New World with refugees from ecclesiastical authorities. It was in North America that people would pioneer a new path to the old goals of harmony and unity. The assumption was that a political dogma promulgated from above could now be dispensed with because mankind, having passed through the turmoils of cultural puberty, was ready to organize itself spontaneously. Mankind (meaning a small slice of the white male population of the North Atlantic basin) was ready to cooperate through the free apprehension of universal truths about rights and other values. These truths were considered universal because they were self-evident—but they were considered self-evident only because they were universal in a highly conditional sense. They were hypothetically universal.

In a remarkable letter to Thomas Law (June 13, 1814), Jefferson responded to Law's treatise *Second Thoughts on Instinctive Impulses,* which dealt with "the foundations of morality in man." Jefferson confessed that he was perplexed on only one point: "It is really curious that on a question so fundamental, such a variety of opinions should have prevailed among men, and those, too, of the most exemplary virtue and first order of understanding."[7]

That is, there are important things that are not self-evident even to civilized men of goodwill. Jefferson, though mildly vexed, refused to be cranky with the Creator for this inconvenience in creation. Indeed, Jefferson complimented Him for it: "It shows how necessary was the care of the Creator in making the moral principle so much a part of our constitution as that no errors of reasoning or of speculation might lead us astray from its observation in practice."[8] Does this mean that men will act well even if they reason poorly? Jefferson notes that "The Creator would indeed have been a bungling artist, had he intended man for a social animal, without planting in him social dispositions."[9] But with regard to such dispositions, God did bungle a bit:

It is true they are not planted in every man, because there is no rule without exceptions. . . . When it is wanting, we endeavor to supply the defect by education, by appeals to reason and calculation, by presenting to the being so unhappily conformed, other motives to endeavor to do good and eschew evil, such as the love, or the hatred, or rejection of those among whom he lives, and whose society is necessary to his happiness and even existence; demonstrations by sound calculation that honesty promotes interest in the long run . . . These are the correctives which are supplied by education.[10]

Jefferson's language is the language of Madison, who in *Federalist* 51 explained the practice of supplying by "interests" the "defect of better motives." Madison was speaking about balanced government. Jefferson used Madisonian phrases to speak about balanced men—the men whom we describe today in totally different language but in identical spirit as "well adjusted" or "socially well rounded." Jefferson said that "nature" (or God—to Jefferson, the difference between God and nature was not, as lawyers say, of constitutional dimension) has "constituted *utility* to man, the standard and test of virtue."[11] And nature enables man to be armed with education—"demonstrations by sound calculation"—that will help supply "social dispositions."

Lincoln and the "naive" doctrine of self-evidence died at about the same time. His rise to greatness was spurred by disgust with Mr. Justice Taney's gloss on the Declaration of Independence' "self-evident" truths in the matter of Dred Scott. Lincoln, the ultimate American, presided over the flaming death of the most American form of serenity, the steady belief in the effortless self-evidence of the political truths animating our liberal democratic order. Robert Penn Warren has captured some of Lincoln's significance:

. . . it even seems that something had happened to the American character between 1776 and 1861. Perhaps the historians are right who say that if we look at the portraits of the Founding Fathers we see faces of men strong, practical, intelligent, and self-assured—and not burdened with excessive sensitivity. But we know that the strength of a

Lincoln or a Grant was a different kind of strength, a strength somehow earned out of inner turmoil.[12]

The faces of both Grant and his Commander bore the marks of lonely struggles to overcome bitter personal disappointments and failures in early life. But more than this, theirs were faces which had seen, close up, the climactic events which taught their countrymen the grim rules of life. President Lincoln, who twice failed to carry his own Sangamon County in Illinois, was acutely aware that any connection between the truth and the electoral success of a political position is highly contingent. Lincoln spoke constantly of the Declaration of Independence, and set the blood flowing and spent 600,000 lives in order that the nation might undergo a rebirth of dedication to the Declaration's central truths. But the very fact that the blood had to flow in unprecedented torrents proved that the Declaration's great truths are not easily self-evident. The principles of free government advocated in Jefferson's Declaration, embodied in the Constitution, expounded in *The Federalist* and defended and ennobled by the life of Lincoln have survived the rigors of two centuries singularly fraught with dangers to political decency. But what the nation learned in Lincoln's lifetime was that the social cohesion which proceeds from shared adherence to a public philosophy and shared emulation of exemplary behavior and values is not the result of spontaneous combustion. It takes work. But by whom, and with what? The answer is: By statecraft that is soulcraft. Such work is done with laws and other institutions. It is the citizenry working on itself—on its self, collectively; on its selves, individually. It is applied political philosophy.

Political philosophy began in Greek city-states. Its origin was urban, and it is a question how much the density of a society can be thinned before the idea of citizenship becomes too attenuated to hold meaning. Perhaps that helps explain why

Lincoln, who lived near the frontier, was so ardent about a sense of citizenship "dedicated" to a defining "proposition." The fact that Americans were not physically close might be compensated for by making them morally close through a crucial shared proposition. Philosophy would supply an intimacy that geography impeded.

Modernity is an urban phenomenon. A pastoral James Joyce is, to say no more, hard to conceive. The city's random sounds and swirls of color symbolize the modern obsession: energy. But the political philosophy of modernity—severe individualism; private self-interestedness made to do duty for public-spirited motives—can produce a yawning social space between citizens. It can produce that even between persons—perhaps especially between persons—who are, in Jefferson's phrase, "piled up in cities." This political philosophy, as it evolved in the seventeenth and eighteenth centuries, provided a justification for government to turn aside from concern for the character of its citizenry. The emergence of the Christian Church, which asserted custody over the inner life of Western man, set the stage for the abdication of state responsibility in that sphere. By the eighteenth century, the abdication was justified without reference to religious responsibilities or any division of labor with other institutions. Rather, it was justified because "unimproved" human nature, with its low but strong desires, was a solid foundation for "the new science of politics." However, toward the end of the nineteenth century there began to be heard a new reason for people to desire a statecraft that makes no attempt at soulcraft. The reason was a growing uncertainty about the very idea of a known or even knowable human nature.

It has been said that we would be well served if thinkers thought less about the history of man's deeds and more about the history of his nature. The most politically important idea of the last two centuries is the idea that human nature has a history. The supposed clarity and certainty of human nature had been a reason for not risking soulcraft: Why alter the "only immutable point in the human heart," the great given from which the political order can take its bearings, the suorce of regularity and predictability and manipulability?

Recently, however, the new reason for not wanting the state engaged in soulcraft has been nervousness. It is nervousness about the very idea of human nature. The individual has an increasingly tenuous sense of his or her "self." The idea of "individuality," the primary preoccupation of modern thought, has become problematic.

A defining oddity of twentieth-century intellectual life and politics is this: As the concept of the "self" has become more problematic, it has become more central in realms of thought and action, in literature and politics. Relatively recently, "consciousness" has become an important term in political vocabularies; "consciousness-raising" has become an important political objective. As individuals have come to feel—have been taught to feel—an increasingly fragile sense of "self," they have become more obsessive and aggressive about "self-expression." There has grown an acute anxiety about the suffocation of the "self" by the modern state with its bureaucratic and communications technologies of social control, and even more by "society." The eighteenth century defined "society" as a friend, or at least as a beneficent mechanism. The twentieth century has defined society as a threat.

Belief in a directing God in the historical process was replaced, in an astonishingly few generations, by what H. L. Mencken called a sense of "the immense indifference of things." The eighteenth-century confidence that the historical process is rational yielded in the nineteenth century to the pervasive sense that the process is not even intelligible. Suddenly, popularized theories held that the process is a swirl of racial impulses, national vitalisms and random events. Theories that made the historical process intelligible made it menacing. Mankind was reduced to potter's clay, spun on a wheel run by Darwinian dynamism, or "iron laws" of Marxian dialectics, or the "cunning" of Hegelian "Reason" that did not seem reasonable.

We are just beginning to understand the extent to which persons are physical mechanisms. There are going to be large changes in mankind's morale as we come to terms with the fact that so many of the things that make us interesting creatures and sustain our self-esteem—our moods, affections and capacities—are matters of chemistry, and at least in theory manipulable by chemicals. This may leave mankind with an even more desiccated sense of identity. But already, in varying degrees, the makers of the modern mind—Darwin, Marx, Freud—either taught or have been construed to have taught that man is, in various ways, passive and plastic to the pressures of his surroundings. Of course, many of the people who most avidly espouse theories explaining why our lives are out of control have in mind political arrangements that would enable them to control us. But for whatever reason, history, physics, biology, psychology and sociology all have been made to seem to teach that man is not free. Darwin, especially, was a great subverter of confidence. This was not just because he asserted, to the detriment of mankind's sense of dignity, the continuity of all protoplasm. It was also because he placed the concept of chance at the center of science, which previously had rested on a conception of nature embodying an exact and predictable design that reason could decipher. The idea that man is a finished product, a polished creation on a pedestal, has been supplanted by the sense that man is a bead on a string—perhaps a very early bead on a very long string.

And in the individual as well as the species, the ratio of being to becoming seems heavily weighted on the side of becoming. If the human condition is one of perpetual becoming, then there is no human nature as commonly conceived: there is instead pure potential. As this sense spread to the arts, an aesthetic of permanence was replaced by an aesthetic of process, of flux, of "becoming." Randomness in composition became both a sign and a doctrine of modern painting. Modern painting and physics conveyed, simultaneously, a sense that reality is without solidity. Van Gogh painted landscapes, even vases of sunflowers, as swirls of energy. Thirty years later, Einstein said that that was realism. With undreamt-of speeds attained on the ground, and with astonishing views from heights (the Eiffel Tower, and then skyscrapers, balloons and airplanes), the great achievement of art since the Renaissance—perspective—suddenly seemed radically inadequate as a means of rendering modern experience. Gertrude Stein wrote of her first flight:

I saw all the lines of cubism made at a time when not any painter had ever gone up in an airplane. I saw there on the earth the mingling lines of Picasso, coming and going, developing and destroying themselves, I saw the simple solutions of Braque, yes I saw and once more I knew that a creator is a contemporary, he understands what is contemporary when the contemporaries do not yet know it, but he is contemporary and as the twentieth century is a century which sees the earth as no-one has ever seen it, the earth has a splendor that it never has had, and as everything destroys itself in the twentieth century and nothing continues, so then the twentieth century has a splendor which is its own.[13]

The splendor of this century is somewhat less amazing today. The charm of destruction has worn off for people who have had to witness so much of it, and who live in an age capable of smashing the atom and everything made of atoms. But the late-nineteenth-century cult of consciousness, or "sensibility," was a desperate assertion of wholeness and autonomy against experiences and theories that seemed to mock both. Sensibility, randomly formed and spontaneously expressed, became a touchstone of modern art. Two other values, "sincerity" and "authenticity," are not actually other values. They are, supposedly, forms spontaneity takes.

The principle of modern manufacturing is the mass production of identical products by means of the assembly of interchangeable parts. The principal anxiety of modern liberalism is the fear of uniformity, usually called conformity. The principal affirmation of modern liberalism is that every individual is a person of many parts, a person who assembles himself or herself. Every individual can be a self-constituting creature, manufacturing himself by choosing purposes and values by whatever principle he wishes from the universe of possibilities. America has led the world with mass manufacturing, and with mass worry about "conformity." The great American novel *The Great Gatsby* is about a work of art: Gatsby's creation of his "self."

The "authenticity" of any self is a function of the free choices made by the individual self-assembler. The integrity of the chosen self is a function of radical resistance to life's givenness, to anything that might "impose" choices. Hence freedom is defined in hostility toward conventions. This notion of what it is to be a free and dignified person contrasts sharply with the notion (set forth by Aristotle, Hegel and others) that man is a social creature, and the value of his life is to some extent a function of his association with persons whose similar moral construction derives from intercourse in a moral community.

A sense of moral community gave rise to a distinctive Victorian earnestness, which many people today find quaint. It reflected confidence in the efficacy of individual effort, and hence confidence that even "under the bludgeoning of chance . . . I am the master of my fate: I am the captain of my soul." But there were multiplying and widening fissures in the intellectual foundations of that confidence.

Between the publication of Darwin's *Origin of Species* in

1859 and the publication in 1893 of *On the Psychological Mechanism of Hysterical Phenomena* by Freud (with Josef Breuer), there was the publication of the first volume of *Das Kapital* (1867). In the span of a generation mankind came face to face with various forms of the idea that change—biological, personal, social—is an autonomous process.

Christianity taught the dependence of mankind on its Creator. But what burst upon the second half of the nineteenth century was a different sense of man's dependency and creatureliness, a sense subversive of mankind's serenity and self-esteem. All of us have been around for as long as we can remember, and probably rather resent the idea that we owe our existence to someone or something else. As Martin Luther is made to say in John Osborne's play about him, "It's hard to accept you're anyone's son, and you're not the father of yourself."[14] But it is one thing to be told that you were created by a majestic and loving God who cares for you individually; it is something very less pleasant to be told that one's species is a product of a series of fortuitous misprints in the transmission of the genetic code. It is not clear what one is believing if one believes that there is God's will in the fall of a sparrow. But whatever one is believing, it is bound to be better than believing, as Marxists must, that the course of history, including the history of human nature, is governed by the iron laws of the development of the means of production. The Christian dichotomy of body and soul, flesh and spirit, may seem increasingly problematic, given what is being learned (and done, pharmacologically) about the chemistry of moods and conduct. But the Christian dichotomy has never been disorienting, as is the fractioning of the self as postulated by modern psychology.

Freud may have been a "reluctant Columbus,"[15] and Columbus was a confused Columbus, which demonstrates that the mental state of a discoverer does not determine the impact of a discovery. Psychology may, or may not, be "the science of candor and scepticism about motives." It certainly is among the underminers of the idea of a unitary, composed self: the self, far from being unitary, is a kind of committee, and a fractious one at that, an arena of strife between instinct and the desire to survive in society. Psychoanalytic models of determinism offer explanations of individuals' behavior, but at the considerable cost of blurring the concept of the individual. By presuming to be the cartography of the dark continent of the subconscious, locating various instincts and feelings, psycho-analysis can purport to explain why John did something, but only by disintegrating our sense—and John's sense—of who, or what, John is.

The idea of personal identity's being problematic was abroad long before Freud postulated the tripartite division of the self. A problem with the sense of "identity" was implicit in Hume's argument that consciousness is a constantly changing kaleido-scope of experiences and impressions—what more recent phi-losophers have called "sense data." Marcel Proust contributed the idea (anticipated by William Wordsworth and others) that the self is a retrospective construct of memory. As Louis MacNeice wrote:

> But I cannot deny my past to which my self is wed,
> The woven figure cannot undo its thread.[16]

Walter Pater used the same image, speaking of "that strange, perpetual weaving and unweaving of ourselves." He, like many contemporaries, thought the self to be the result of ran-dom and evanescent forces: ". . . those impressions of the individual mind to which, for each one of us, experience dwindles down, are in perpetual flight; that each of them is limited by time, and that as time is infinitely divisible, each of them is infinitely divisible also; all that is actual in it being a single moment, gone while we try to apprehend it, of which it may ever be more truly said that it has ceased to be than that it is."[17]

Experience in perpetual flight, mind dwindling down—this is a description of insecurity at the core of existence. This insecurity has bred peculiar assertions and defiances that are forms of bravado in the face of anxiety. D. H. Lawrence ("Be a good animal, true to your instincts.")[18] exemplified the flight from intellect to a cult of experience, in the name of freedom: "The world doesn't fear a new idea. It can pigeonhole any idea. But it can't pigeonhole a new experience."[19] In politics as well as culture, liberalism has become a doctrine of "liberation," often understood as willfulness. As a result, much modern art substitutes mere will for objective achievement. And sex, art, even education have become vehicles for "self-expression." Education is "self-expression"? That is an idea comparable to Oscar Wilde's thought that punctuality is the thief of time. The feeling that the self is an embattled entity struggling for expression in a suffocating society gave rise to the alienated figure prominent in modern literature, standing at the margin of, and often in opposition to, society. This figure expresses what Lionel Trilling called modernism's "bitter line of hostility toward civilization."[20]

In art, Impressionism set the agenda for much that followed: the painter's subject was not what he saw but the act of seeing. "Painting from Nature," Paul Cézanne said, "is not copying the object; it is realizing one's sensations."[21] He said, "The same subject seen from a different angle gives a motif of the highest interest, and so varied that I think I could be occupied for months without changing my place—simply bending a little more to the right or left."[22] That is fine if you are "realizing" your "sensations" in rural Provence, gazing at Mt. Ste. Victoire, as Cézanne forever was. But at about this time art became urban. Just as the cityscape was replacing the landscape as the dominant image in painting, "society" was beginning to seem like a problem. By the middle of this century Mark Rothko would write: "The familiar identity of things has to be pulverized in order to destroy the finite sensations with which our society increasingly enshrouds every aspect of our environment."[23] By suffocating our capacity for infinite sensations, society leaves us with a withered "self," because the "self" is nothing but sensations. It was in that spirit that French students, during the 1968 disturbances, painted on Paris walls the slogan *"La société est une fleur carnivore."* Gauguin taking his "primitive blood" to Tahiti and T. E. Lawrence enjoying the "barbarians" of the desert were after the purity of natural sensation. It was an echo of Shelley's dream of man "sceptreless, free, uncircumscribed . . . equal, unclassed, tribeless, and nationless, exempt from awe, worship, degree, the King over himself."[24] As D. H. Lawrence wrote, "If you are walking westward . . . you forfeit the northern and eastward and southern directions. If you admit a unison, you forfeit all the possibilities of chaos."[25]

D. H. Lawrence's longing for the possibilities of chaos was eccentric, but Americans, who arrived not long ago on an empty continent—the closest thing to a social *tabula rasa* that civilized man ever enjoyed—have only reluctantly surrendered their belief in infinite possibility. The persistent melancholy beneath the skin of American life derives from the unavoidable knowledge that the circumference of the sphere of possibility narrows as society matures. "Providence," said De Tocqueville, "has not created mankind entirely independent or entirely free. It is true that around every man a fatal circle is traced beyond which he cannot pass; but within the wide verge of that circle he is powerful and free."[26] Americans have insistently sought the widest possible verge. Lincoln's life expressed the essence of American aspiration not because he went West to the wilderness but because, as the campaign song said, "Old Abe Lincoln came out of the wilderness." He came out and conquered the East. Woodrow Wilson said Lincoln owed nothing to his birth, everything to his growth. Lincoln is hardly typical, but his myth exemplifies an American longing for personal "growth" unshaped by "society." Where better to grow than on the prairie stretching (in Whitman's words) "on its own undaunted scale, unconfined"?

An American dream is to be unconfined by geography or history. Ralph Waldo Emerson, an American archetype, considered himself "an endless seeker with no Past at my back." And his idea of satisfactory education was the self-education of the Thoreau boys who had "gone up the Merrimack to live by their wits."[27] The oldest American romance is with the idea of a pathless wilderness in which absolute individualism—what is today called "self-realization"—is uninhibited by social bonds. But must we always speak of society in connection with the nasty word "bonds"? The word suggests ropes biting into wrists. We have come out of the wilderness, into society, where we belong. But intellectually, in terms of political philosophy, we are still up the Merrimack. It is time to come up from individualism. We have had quite enough Leatherstocking Tales, thank you. We need a literature of cheerful sociability, novels of social "thickness" that make society seem a complex but friendly place where social relationships facilitate rather than frustrate individualism and "self-realization." And we need a public philosophy that can rectify the current imbalance between the political order's meticulous concern for material well-being and its fastidious withdrawal from concern for the inner lives and moral character of citizens. In fine, we must rethink today's constricted notion of the legitimate uses of law.

CHAPTER FOUR

Second Nature

> By wholesome laws to embank the sovereign power,
> To deepen by restraint, and by prevention
> Of Lawless will to amass and guide the flood
> In its majestic channel, is man's task
> And the true patriot's glory!
>   —SAMUEL TAYLOR COLERIDGE

A POLITY is not a building, begun with an identifiable plunge of a spade into earth and completed at a particular time. A polity is a river of constantly changing composition, and the river's banks are built of laws. "Government," as Burke said, "is a contrivance of human wisdom to provide for human *wants*," and among these wants is "a sufficient restraint upon their passions."[1] Freedom is not only the absence of external restraints. It also is the absence of irresistible internal compulsions, unmanageable passions and uncensorable appetites. From the need to resist, manage and censor the passions there flows the need to do so in the interest of some ends rather than others. Hence freedom requires reflective choice about the ends of life.

The ends must be related to what is given at the "beginning." But fewer human attributes—passions, desires, inclinations—arise from "nature," as opposed to convention, than used to be assumed. The ancient understanding of philosophy as the attempt to discover nature, and especially human nature, has been complicated, if not undermined, by the modern idea that human nature has a history. This modern idea is to be distinguished from the older idea that human nature, once pure, has been corrupted in this or that way. Rather, the modern idea is the more radical—perhaps the ultimate radical—idea: the idea that there is no "essential" human nature. If that were true, one familiar strand of radicalism would be refuted. The refuted belief would be the utopian notion that we can recover the "essential," the "uncorrupted" human nature by purging society of this or that corrupting influence (private property, or self-love, or cities, or whatever). Such a utopian program certainly is mistaken; but so too is the notion that new knowledge has rendered the very idea of human nature anachronistic. The social sciences, psychology and other disciplines have enriched our understanding of the extent to which persons are creatures of convention. But nothing yet learned or likely to be learned has justified or will justify the conclusion that human conventions account for everything. Instead of juxtaposing nature and convention, for the purpose of defining the domain of each, the old question of political philosophy is still the right question: What kinds of conventions are especially suited to human nature?

Madison and the other Founders asked the correct question, but they gave an answer that requires amendment. Their conception of the politically relevant human nature was too stark, too unidimensional in its emphasis on self-interestedness. The urgency of the complaint against Madison's answer derives from the fact that political philosophy is a political act; a conception of human nature can be somewhat self-fulfilling. It is especially apt to be so when, as in this nation, institutional arrangements and numerous public policies conform to that conception.

Political arrangements can be said to be suitable when they suit human nature as modified by the habits of the citizens who live with the arrangements. But a function of government is the modification of habits. "Politics," said Burke, "ought to be adjusted not to human reasonings, but to human nature."[2] But law is a subject of reasoning, and law—and thus politics—helps us with our "second nature." The "second nature" is not an overlay, a kind of varnish spread on top of the "first nature." Rather, it is a conscious recovery of, and enhancement of, a portion of the first nature, the "given" in human beings. Saying somewhat the same thing similarly, George Santayana wrote: "A native country is a sort of second body, another enveloping organism to give the will definition."[3]

Now, it is not very illuminating to say, for example, that immigrants flooded through Ellis Island because the United States suited their essential human nature better than did, say, nineteenth-century Poland. When the Indochinese "boat people" put to sea, putting everything at risk, they were fleeing a system that frustrated many of the fundamental aspirations, tendencies, capabilities of normal people. The East German regime had to build a wall to lock in its population because its population was attracted to the West, where they could find scope to realize those fundamental aspirations, tendencies, capabilities. One is not committed to much in the way of specific political arrangements when one speaks of such fundamental things. However, speaking of them is a way to begin the long march to political understanding.

Begin at the outer edges of the awful. Begin from circumstances that are so intolerable that they drive many persons to desperation. Then work in, by small inferences, toward an understanding of political excellence. Along the way, much will be learned about how excellence is related to essential human traits—the very traits thwarted by inhuman regimes. No one denies that there are some characteristic human nonphysical traits. A sociopath is someone who is, for whatever reasons, lacking in some of the moral or psychological or spiritual traits. A concentration-camp guard is perhaps apt to be, strictly speaking, inhuman, in that some of those traits have been suppressed or erased.

When we see a playground teeming with unformed kindergartners, we may well think: Gosh! There are all sorts of possibilities. But are there? *All* sorts? Perhaps we who believe in a "first nature," but who also believe the evidence of our senses and of this century, must believe that it is at least theoretically possible that "anything is possible"—that the mass of mankind could be pounded and ground into any shape. The radical degradation of large numbers of persons—if not whole societies—has occurred. Still, the most one must say is: Perhaps anything can happen—but not soon; not on short order; not predictably.

The denial that there is an essential human nature can take many forms. Hegel, for example, did not believe in an essential human nature, but he did believe that the evolution of human consciousness proceeds by an autonomous, decipherable process. Furthermore, there is only meager nourishment for political philosophy from the mere idea that there is an essential human nature. However, the denial of that idea leaves political philosophy dangerously unmoored. And denial does not at all emancipate the denier from the duty to think about soulcraft. For persons in the broad natural-law tradition, the word "law" refers to certain fundamental facts about the world that help determine right and wrong acts and arrangements. Such persons believe they have a navigational aid—a kind of compass—on the political journey. But persons who accept the premise of modernity are not thereby freed from the need to practice soulcraft. On the contrary, logic and prudence should compel them to feel specially committed to statecraft as soulcraft. If mankind is utterly plastic to circumstances, that is a powerful reason for taking care to shape circumstances with political needs in mind. If a human being is, except for a few strong forms of animal spirits, a *tabula rasa*, then an urgent task of citizenship is to see that the civic system does some careful writing on the blank slate.

The concept "law" can involve two different things—observed regularities, or norms to which persons ought to choose to conform. The classic theory of natural law involves the latter; it is prescriptive, not descriptive. The idea of "the natural" connotes an imperative more general and durable than the particular needs of a particular community at the moment. Classical natural-law theory holds that there is a characterizing excellence of which man is capable. This end toward which he should strive is knowable through reason. It is not, in fact, universally understood. But it is, in theory, universally understandable.

The philosophical problems with this theory have been adumbrated for centuries: How do you identify the characterizing essence of a category of creatures, such as man? How do you derive an "ought" (an obligation to pursue a particular end, called excellence) from an "is" (the fact—if it is such—that man has a characterizing essence)? These philosophic problems are real. But so is the persistent human tendency to talk as though the crux of natural-law theory were common sense. Listen to the logic of common language: about goals that are naturally worthy, about the proper values for civilized people, about behavior that is inhuman. The logic of our moral discourse suggests dependency on a structure of assumptions similar to those of classical natural-law theory.

This does not, of course, clinch any philosophic point. It is not intellectually satisfying, or philosophically permissible, to argue the truth of a proposition because of the social utility of acting as though the proposition were true. But it is reasonable to note that we serve good governance by acting on the assumptions that underlie our moral language.

Steadily and rapidly, for forty years, society has become more politicized, in the sense that state action has come increasingly to influence the allocation of wealth and opportunity. But there has been an interestingly simultaneous decline in the efforts of the political agencies to influence society's values. Numerous changes in laws—liberalization, virtually to elimination, of obscenity laws; liberalization of abortion laws to abortion-on-demand; elimination of most laws criminalizing sexual activity among consenting adults; prohibition of many compulsory and even some voluntary political and religious affirmations or observances in public places (flag salutes and prayers in schools, Christmas crèches on public property)—are evidence of the steady withdrawal of the law from concern with the citizenry's state of mind. All this may have been implicit in the premises of political modernity which the Founders frequently preached. But the society the Founders lived in—the society that preceded the nation; the society that produced the Founders—did not practice the modernity the Founders preached. And the Founders sometimes preached something other than thoroughgoing modernity.

George Washington, in his Farewell Address, called religion indispensable for "all the dispositions and habits which lead to political prosperity." That is less important as an empirical proposition about the utility of religion than as a thought about the indispensability of particular character traits.

Writing in favor of religious toleration, Jefferson said something quoted and admired today: ". . . it does me no injury for my neighbor to say there are twenty gods, or no God. It neither picks my pocket nor breaks my leg."[4] Yet in the same essay (*Notes on Virginia*) he wrote: "And can liberties of a nation be thought secure when we have removed their only firm basis, a conviction in the minds of the people that these liberties are the gift of God? That they are not to be violated but with His wrath?"[5] How can religious convictions, or their absence, be a matter of indifference if the liberty of the nation— and hence the safety of his pocketbook and even his limbs—

depends on a particular conviction? Whether Jefferson is correct about the connection between the security of liberty and the prevalence of a particular conviction is an empirical question, and perhaps still an open one. But the logic of his position is awkward, as is the logic of modern politics generally.

Whatever else Americans have from time to time included among their goals, they always have included the universalizing of material comfort. To that end, the New Deal altered, fundamentally, the relationship of the citizen to the national government. It did so by asserting that government's responsibility for a distributive role in providing for "welfare," defined as material well-being. The almost limitless expansion of American government since the New Deal, which corresponds to the expansion of welfare states throughout the industrial world, was implicit in the commission given to government by modern political philosophy: the commission to increase pleasure and decrease pain. The expansion is only "almost" limitless, because government has actually been contracting in the sphere of concern for the cultivation of character or virtue. This, too, is implicit in the turn taken by political philosophy four centuries ago. But surely there is a middle ground between the ancient belief in a connection between human perfectibility and the political order, and the modern belief in the political order as merely an instrument for coming to terms with human imperfections. In fact, modern actions often speak not only louder but more sensibly than modern words. Liberal democratic societies have generally governed themselves more sensibly than they have described or explained themselves regarding concern for the "inner life of man." American society has expressed such concern by investing vast resources, and extravagant hopes, in education.

Americans have always been an "improving" people, given to associating for the purpose of purifying their souls or refining their talents. The Chautauqua tent, along with a piece of collegiate gothic, should stand as symbols of the American's humble but steady passion for improvement. But the central symbol would be the little red schoolhouse, standing for public education.

In case after case, the Supreme Court has emphasized—taught—that education has a "fundamental role in maintaining the fabric of our society"[6] and a "pivotal role" in "sustaining our political and cultural heritage."[7] In the most consequential "teaching" decision of the modern age, the Court described education as "the very foundation of good citizenship . . . a principal instrument in awakening the child to cultural values."[8] The Court has insisted that the "public school is a most vital civic institution for the preservation of a democratic system of government"[9] and the primary instrument for transmitting "the values on which our society rests."[10] The Court's reiterated teaching on this subject is part cause and part effect of the traditional "perception of the public school as inculcating fundamental values necessary to the maintenance of a democratic system."[11] In such statements the Court has been uncommonly faithful to the intentions of the Founders.

John Adams admonished his fellow Founders that "whoever would found a state, and make proper laws for the government of it, must presume that all men are bad by nature." But Adams tempered his dourness with the most soothingly American confidence: "Human nature with all its infirmities and depravities is still capable of great things. . . . Education makes a greater difference between man and man, than nature has made between man and brute. The virtues and powers to which men may be trained, by early education and constant discipline, are truly sublime and astonishing."[12]

The First Congress readopted the Northwest Ordinance passed first by the Continental Congress in 1787. The Third Article, pertaining to land for schools, declared: "Religion, morality, and knowledge, being necessary to good government

and the happiness of mankind, schools and the means of learning shall forever be encouraged."[13]

By 1745 there were three colleges in British North America.
There were seven more by 1776, and nearly every Christian
sect had or had arranged financial support for an institution
of its own.[14] American higher education has been a high-
growth industry for well over a century, in part because of the
"booster colleges" founded by struggling new American communities west of the Appalachians, where the presence of a
college or university was supposed to lend communities a
semblance of, and thereby promote, that elusive American goal
of permanence. "Of the one hundred eighty-odd colleges and
universities founded in these years [between the Revolution
and the Civil War] which survived into the 20th century, well
over a hundred appeared outside the original thirteen colonies.
. . . By 1880, President Frederick A. P. Bernard of Columbia
was wondering how England, with a population of twenty-
three million, managed with four degree granting institutions,
while the state of Ohio, with a population of only three million,
supplied thirty-seven."[15]

Today, California's Constitution states: "A general diffusion
of knowledge and intelligence being essential to the preservation of the rights and liberties of the people, the Legislature
shall encourage by all suitable means the promotion of intellectual, scientific, moral and agricultural improvement."[16] It is not
only amusing, it is significant that California sandwiches moral
improvement between scientific and agricultural improvement.
Americans have always been inclined to believe that an idle
brain is the Devil's playground, and that busy hands make a
good heart, and that if people are equipped to be productive,
they will be good citizens.

In 1787, the year the Constitutional Convention met to "revise" the Articles of Confederation, the task of constituting the
country was just beginning, and Jefferson was in Paris, where

the deconstituting of the *ancien régime* was about to begin. He wrote in a private letter: "The basis of our governments being the opinion of the people, the very first object should be to keep that right."[17] But in 1801, at the conclusion of his First Inaugural Address, Jefferson said: "Still one thing more, fellow citizens—a wise and frugal government, which shall restrain men from injuring one another, which shall leave them otherwise free to regulate their own pursuits of industry and improvements, and shall not take from the mouth of labor the bread it has earned. This is the sum of good government, and this is necessary to close the circle of our felicities."[18] The "sum"? Is that all it takes? No, not even if all components of the crucial consensus are "self-evident" to unclouded minds. Good government must promote the proliferation of such minds.

By 1820, Jefferson had been President for two terms (an accomplishment he thought not important enough to warrant mention on his tombstone) and had established the University of Virginia (the third of the three accomplishments cited on his tombstone, the others being the authorship of the Declaration of Independence and the Virginia Declaration of Human Rights). In 1820 he wrote: "I know of no safe depository of the ultimate powers of the society but the people themselves, and if we think them not enlightened enough to exercise their control with a wholesome discretion, the remedy is not to take it from them but to inform their discretion by education."[19] But education to inform discretion has often seemed less important than the sort of education encouraged by the political philosophy of modernity: that is, education for a republic in which passions are absorbed by commerce; education to equip the individual for efficacious self-interestedness.

Jefferson said it was an "axiom" of his mind that liberty is safe only in the hands of the people, but the people require "a certain degree of instruction. This it is the business of the state to effect on a general plan."[20] In 1827, one year after the death of Jefferson (whose Louisiana Purchase should have been a fourth accomplishment mentioned on his tombstone), John Marshall wondered "as our country fills up how shall we escape the evils which have followed on dense population?"[21] He asserted that "education—that degree of education which is adapted to the wants of the laboring class, and which prevails generally in the United States—especially in those of the north— is the surest preservative of the morals and the comforts of human life."[22] In 1862, the Morrill Act was passed, giving rise to the land-grant college system. One of the first such colleges grew like Topsy and today is Michigan State University, whose seal still proclaims the original purposes of the undertaking: "Agriculture and Applied Science." Those are the two fields of "improvement" which California's Constitution mentions before and after "moral improvement."

But education, understood (perhaps generously) as what schools do, is not sufficient. The law must be a tutor in other ways.

Plato said that successful reform depended on banishing everyone more than ten years old. Parents may sometimes think Plato got that backward, but students of political philosophy will recognize Plato's theme as one that recurs often in Western political philosophy. It is the wistful dream of a social *tabula rasa*. It is, of course, an idle dream. "Did one generation of men go off the stage at once, and another succeed, as is the case with silkworms and butterflies," wrote David Hume, "the new race . . . might voluntarily . . . establish their own form of civil polity without any regard to the laws or precedents, which prevailed among their ancestors."[23] But persons are not silkworms (or, in Burke's words, "flies of summer"). They are products of the laws under which they are raised and live, and of the long legacy of their culture.

Surely there is nothing shocking about the idea that society's

institutions are concrete embodiments of social values which
can claim precedence over the desire of the individual or even
the collective will of the moment. No one disputes that a social
order embodies certain values, or that law intimates purposes
beyond itself. Law, obviously, has the important task of guaran-
teeing the minimal outward conformity with duties necessary
for a liberal order. Law counteracts the diversities of a people,
requiring at least the minimal harmony required for social
peace. But those diversities which necessitate law also necessitate law concerned with values as well as actions—with mind as
well as body. They necessitate law as a ratifier and stigmatizer,
in which role law is a tutor.

Once it was thought sufficient for a citizen to "belong" to a
polity by sharing its protection and prosperity. In the modern
age, the idea of "belonging" involves the added dimension of
participation in governance. Hence, the idea of tutelary government has become especially problematic. But sound laws do
not rule people; sound laws help nurture the fabric of assumptions and disciplines by which people rule themselves. Therefore, law must pay attention to the imperatives of culture, and
must occasionally counter them with imperatives of its own.
Hume was, of course, right: "All plans of government which
suppose great reformation in the manners of mankind are
plainly imaginary."[24] When Rousseau said that we must establish censors when the laws are strong, he understood this point:
The husbandry of virtue can succeed only when it is not especially urgent—when, that is, the danger of dissolution is not
clear and present.

Therein lies the problem. How do you educate a comfortable, complacent society to do what is complicated, difficult, dangerous if done wrong and necessary only in the long
run? This is a society rather too fond of the *mot* that in the
long run we are all dead. The author of that sentiment—
Keynes—was, of course, childless. Parents do not think that

way. The great conservatizing experience is having children. Raising them teaches adults the scale of the task of creating citizens from raw—very raw—material. It also teaches adults how much this most important of all social tasks is a task of transmission. Parents and schools are primarily instruments for transmitting what others have acquired for us. Thus, bringing up children teaches the teachers a lesson about the cumulativeness of life. It also teaches that renunciation of the instinctual life is, as Freud said, a price of civilization. And the price is paid, in part, in the coin of law.

The "fundamental law," as the Constitution is called, is fundamental because it is a foundation. A foundation is something on which an edifice rests. The word "rest" is barely in the social lexicon of this restless nation. Go West, go "up," get going and keep going—that has been the American spirit. And when everything and everyone is in flux, nothing will be automatically passed on intact to the future. The primary business of conservatism is preservation of the social order that has grown in all its richness—not preserving it like a fly in amber, but protecting it especially from suffocation or dictated alteration by the state. However, the state has a central role to play. The preservation of a nation requires a certain minimum moral continuity, because a nation is not just "territory" or "physical locality." A nation is people "associated in agreement with respect to justice." And continuity cannot be counted on, absent precautions.

When we require legislators and Presidents to swear allegiance to the Constitution, are we really asking only that they pledge allegiance to a system of "change"? Americans have generally assumed that "change" means "growth," which implies health. But even if, in the ninth decade of the twentieth century, that equation is accepted, it does not settle this question: What does the Constitution constitute? It constitutes a polity, a nation, which is more than an institutional arrange-

ment for perpetual openness or "change." It would be quixotic
and imprudent for a community to attempt to freeze its customs, habits and dispositions. But it would be imprudent and
probably fatal to a community to deny the community any
right to attempt to perpetuate itself in recognizable form.

The Constitution does not just distribute powers, it does so
in a cultural context of principles and beliefs and expectations
about the appropriate social outcome of the exercise of those
powers. Only a few of those are even intimated in the text of
the Constitution. That is why, considered apart from the
cultural context, the Constitution is impossible to explicate.
Holmes's famous statement that a constitution "is made for
people of fundamentally differing views"[25] is radically false. A
constitution not only presupposes a consensus of "views" on
fundamentals; it also presupposes concern for its own continuance. Therefore, it presupposes efforts to predispose rising
generations to the "views" and habits and dispositions that
underlie institutional arrangements. In this sense, a constitution
is not only an allocator of powers: it is also the polity's frame
of mind.

Ethics and politics, welded together by Aristotle and the
ancients, have been pried apart by moderns who argue that
legislators must not allow their "private" ethics to intrude upon
the political task, which is merely to provide for the satisfaction of mankind's common desires, such as the desires for life,
liberty and the pursuit of happiness. Burke, almost alone among
modern philosophers, says: "The principles of true politics are
those of morality enlarged."[26] But a prudent legal system will
respect Professor Lon Fuller's distinction between the morality
of aspiration and the morality of duty.

The morality of aspiration "is the morality of the Good Life,
of excellence, of the fullest realization of human powers."[27]
When a man fails to achieve all that to which he aspires, he has
failed, but he has not been "recreant to duty." He is guilty of

a shortcoming, but not of wrongdoing. The morality of duty is less demanding but is also more severe in its judgments.

> Where the morality of aspiration starts at the top of human achievement, the morality of duty starts at the bottom. It lays down the basic rules without which an ordered society is impossible, or without which an ordered society directed toward certain specific goals must fail of its mark. It is the morality of the Old Testament and the Ten Commandments. It speaks in terms of "thou shalt not," and, less frequently, of "thou shalt." It does not condemn men for failing to embrace opportunities for the fullest realization of their powers. Instead, it condemns them for failing to respect the basic requirements of social living.[28]

The crucial words are "directed toward certain specific goals." The morality of duty is enforced on all persons equally. But this is not just to facilitate the "private" pursuit of a morality of aspiration by all citizens, equally, if they are so inclined. Rather, the morality of duty is enforced also to sustain social programs that cannot be reduced to expressions of individual rights. The morality of aspiration governs man's activities beyond social duties he shares with other citizens. The morality of aspiration—a standard of excellence—governs these aspirations by asking, with regard to each activity: Is this "an activity worthy of man's capacities"? The morality of duty governs man the citizen, while the morality of aspiration governs man as he tries to cope excellently with "the broader responsibilities of the human role"—that is, with responsibilities related to the broad possibilities of life beyond the perimeters of the political sphere.

The distinction between the morality of duty and the morality of aspiration expresses the impossibility, or unwisdom, of trying to affect a fusion, in theory or in fact, between the good man and the good citizen. As Fuller sees it, "There is no way by which the law can compel a man to live up to the excellences of which he is capable. For workable standards of judgment the law must turn to its blood cousin, the morality of duty."[29] Fuller argues that "what the morality of aspiration loses in direct relevance for the law, it gains in the pervasiveness of its implications."[30] From the "centuries old struggle to reduce the role of the irrational in human affairs," Fuller draws the lesson that

> there is no way open to us by which we can compel a man to live the life of reason. We can only seek to exclude from his life the grosser and more obvious manifestations of chance and irrationality. We can create the conditions essential for a rational human existence. These are the necessary, but not the sufficient conditions for the achievement of that end.[31]

Fuller says that there is no way to "compel" a man to live the life of reason. But between compulsion and indifference stands a broad area of persuasion, incentives and other noncoercive encouragements to better living. Statesmanlike practice involves locating the region of probable success in bringing citizens, through law, to worthy lives:

> As we consider the whole range of moral issues, we may conveniently imagine a kind of scale or yardstick which begins at the bottom with the obvious demands of social living and extends upward to the highest reaches of human aspiration. Somewhere along this scale there is an invisible pointer that marks the dividing line where the pressure of duty leaves off and the challenge of excellence begins. The whole field of moral argument is dominated by a great undeclared war over the location of this pointer.[32]

Actually, modern political thought has aimed for an armistice in that wholesome war. It has aimed to minimize the pressure of duty applied by government. It has argued for confining government to low and narrow purposes which can be

achieved by orienting politics to mankind's low but steady
passions. It would maximize "freedom," understood as a passionate way of life. What makes Fuller's use of the distinction
between the two moralities especially useful for today is that
it is compatible with the sort of skepticism about ethics that is
often a part of the liberal temper. Fuller vigorously rejects the
idea that "In order to judge what is bad in human conduct, we
must know what is perfectly good."[33] Thus the morality of
aspiration need not be the foundation of all morality, and men
can achieve a political arrangement—a consensus on social
duties—without first achieving consensus on the upper reaches
of human aspiration. The moral injunction "Thou shalt not kill"
implies no picture of the perfect life. It rests on the prosaic
truth that if men kill one another promiscuously, no conceiv-
able morality of aspiration can be realized. In no field of human endeavor is it true that our judgments as to what is un-
desirable must be secretly directed by some half-perceived
utopia.

"The morality of aspiration has to do with our efforts to
make the best use of our short lives," Fuller says.[34] A Hobbesian, glancing nervously over his shoulder at a constantly
looming state of nature, might hold that the morality of duty
has to do only with making our short lives a little less short.
But clearly it is not that simple; clearly the morality of duty
concerns more than maintaining our physical selves in safety
and, exigencies permitting, in some comfort. The beginning of
wisdom should be the recognition that the crucial problem
of political philosophy is not deciding how far the morality of
duty needs to extend, but rather deciding how far it dares to
extend. That is, the aim should not be to cramp and minimize
as much as possible the law's expression of a morality of duty,
but rather to extend it as far as is reasonable to facilitate and
encourage the citizens' practice of the morality of aspiration.

John Stuart Mill's famous formulation was: "The only purpose for which power can rightfully be exercised over any member of a civilized community against the will is to prevent harm to others." And: "His own good, either physical or moral, is not a sufficient warrant."[35] But that is not especially helpful, and neither is the distinction between "self-regarding" and "other-regarding" acts. That distinction is not where the argument ends: it is where analysis begins. The question of what affects others is, perhaps, an empirical question, although often not a simple one. The question of what harms them is even more complex, and involves moral judgment about empirical evidence. The law should not be concerned with "private" moral choices, if by that we designate choices that are not injurious to any other individual or any public interest. But "sufficient warrant" for society to act through law is significant injury to society. Obviously it would be untenable to argue that there can be no such thing as purely private moral choices. But it is equally mistaken to dismiss the possibility that changed patterns of moral choices can have large and intolerable social consequences.

The idea that moral change can produce political and social declines has been ridiculed as comparable to Justinian's belief that homosexuality causes earthquakes. The ridiculers assert that historians can "prove" no causal connection between any examples of moral change and social decline, and that current events offer no convincing evidence. I have no desire to debate here the standards of evidence and proof. Besides, such a debate would approach the problem from the wrong direction. The right approach is with such questions as these: Would those people who deny that law should seek to shape morals also deny that morals shape law? Given that the law is shaped as well as shaping, is it not reasonable that law should be concerned with its social and cultural roots? /Have they all been mistaken, all the philosophers and statesmen from Plato to the present, who have argued that particular forms of government have social and cultural prerequisites, including shared ideas, values and character traits in the citizenry? If a society wills just laws, should it not will the means—the moral prerequisites—to the end?

Modern political philosophy argues that government exists at the initiative of individuals, and generally by the resentful sufferance of individuals, and for the material benefit of individuals here and now. Given the constricted grammar of politics which that philosophy produces, it is hard for laws regulating "personal" behavior to speak of "the interests of society." Nevertheless, the following seems fair.

Intelligent persons of goodwill can disagree as to whether the radical revision of abortion laws since 1973 was wise. But it is impudent of those who think so, and who worked tenaciously to bring this about by judicial fiat, to argue that those who disagree and want to restore the rights of states to regulate abortions are guilty of wanting to "impose" their "personal" values on society. What do the triumphant advocates of the social policy of abortion-on-demand think they have done? They have used judicial power to strike down laws that embodied the democratically expressed judgments of all fifty states. The pro-abortion people have used that power to revise the laws to express their moral judgments. Similarly, it is passing strange that those who have labored so long and skillfully to liberate pornographers from all legal restraints are now cross about those persons who favor less liberation, accusing them of trying to intrude their "private" values into public policy. An individual getting regularly drunk on gin may be a private matter. Millions of workers and parents' regularly getting drunk on gin is a social disaster—and was a reason for the British licensing laws. The law can treat, say, all sales of pornography as private transactions between particular sellers and buyers. But the law cannot make the results—a multibillion-dollar pornography industry; Times Square; the coarsening of many persons' sensibilities; the laceration of the sensibilities of other persons unavoidably bombarded by pornography; dubiety about the very idea of shamefulness, and we know not what else—the law cannot make these results matters of merely private rather than public importance. Similarly, the law can treat abortions as private transactions between women and their doctors. But the law cannot make the consequences—1.7 million abortions a year; a new casualness about the conceiving and disposing of life; transformed attitudes about sex, and hence about relations between the sexes, and the claims of family and children, and we know not what else—the law cannot make them "private" consequences. I say "we know not what else" because we can be certain there will be consequences we cannot anticipate. Society is like a Calder mobile. Touch it here, it trembles over there. Beliefs, habits, mores, dispositions are connected to one another in subtle ways and are related to behavior in many ways. Many of the ways are not known—cannot be known—until a chain of changes has begun.

I do not want to argue here that, say, abortion is right or wrong, only that the question of abortion should be part of society's political argument, and that it is profoundly wrong to try to exclude the abortion issue on the ground that it involves only "private values." Similarly, in the next chapter, I do not argue that capitalism is or is not the glorious thing that its hymnists say it is; but I do say why it is folly to try to seal off all arguments about "economic choices" from political, meaning moral, choices.

Any argument about the legislation of morality comes, sooner or later, and usually immediately, to the matter of Prohibition. The most lasting of the various ill effects of Prohibition has been the use of that "experiment" as evidence to support the facile assertion that "You cannot legislate morality." That assertion is true in the same sense that it is true that "You can't teach virtue." That is, the only thing the law generally can attempt to do with immediately verifiable results is attempt to alter behavior. And it cannot do that when it is opposed to the deep-seated habits and dispositions of a people. (However much Prohibitionists sprang from conservative religious and regional groups, it was an act of radicalism.) In such a case, laws are bound to be what Hobbes called "cob-web laws."

But the enforcement of law, by making visible and sometimes vivid the community values that are deemed important enough to support by law, can bolster these values. "The sentence of the law," said Sir James Fitzjames Stephen, "is to the moral sentiment of the public in relation to any offense what a seal is to hot wax. It converts into a permanent final judgment what otherwise might be a transient sentiment."[36] Of course, nothing in a society, least of all moral sentiment, is permanent and final. Indeed, there have been occasions when the law rightfully set out to change important and passionately held sentiments, and the law proved to be a web of iron.

Before Lester Maddox was Governor of Georgia, he was proprietor of the Pickrick Restaurant in Atlanta. One of the most defensible, indeed most unmixedly good, deeds of modern government was in taking away one of the rights Maddox valued most. When black persons tried to claim a right to be served in the Pickrick, the proprietor responded by wielding an ax handle, and by handing out ax handles to kindred spirits. The right he was exercising was a real right—an enforceable entitlement, and an old one: the right of a proprietor to restrict his custom. In many times and places the right was, and is, acceptable. But in the United States it had too often been exercised in a way that affronted an entire class of citizens. And in the United States in 1964 that right had become intolerably divisive. So Congress undertook a small but significant rearrangement of American rights. It diminished the rights of proprietors of public accommodations, and expanded those of potential users of those accommodations. In explaining why this rearrangement was necessary, Lyndon Johnson said it was because "a man has a right not to be insulted in public in front of his children." No one was concerned with interstate commerce, although the language of the Constitution compelled the pretense that commerce was the governmental interest legitimizing an exercise of power. The simple truth is that in 1964, because of brave and skillful symbolic actions by civil rights forces shaping public opinion, an American majority was unusually aroused and conscious of what Congress was doing. Congress was coming to the conclusion that a right exercised meanly, with ugly consequences, should yield to another, better right.

The great civil rights legislation of the 1960s was, of course, designed primarily to improve the condition of the descendants of slaves. But it had another purpose. It was supposed to do what it in fact did. It was supposed to alter the operation of the minds of many white Americans. The most admirable achievements of modern liberalism—desegregation, and the civil rights acts—were explicit and successful attempts to change (among other things) individuals' moral beliefs by compelling them to change their behavior. The theory was that if government compelled people to eat and work and study and play together, government would improve the inner lives of those people.

Jefferson distinguished "operations of the mind" from "acts of the body" because the former are not "subject to coercion of the laws."[37] But operations of the mind are supposed to precede and cause certain acts. Visible behavior derives from invisible attributes. And it is not too much to hope that enforced patterns of behavior can alter the moral attributes of citizens. To a gratifying extent the civil rights laws worked. We should be proud that our government, which has had many material successes (TVA, the Manhattan Project, the interstate highway system, the Apollo program), has "built" a moral achievement of such great scale. Unfortunately, the political philosophy of modernity has given us a bad conscience about such good works. We are supposed to take our political bearings from what is given "inside" mankind, and accommodate it. We are supposed to believe that (as Felix Frankfurter said, and for reasons Hobbes and Locke and others gave) "law is concerned with external behavior and not the inner life of man."[38] Fortunately, the two realms are connected in potentially useful ways.

But then, everything is connected to everything else. "Social condition," as Alexis de Tocqueville said, "is commonly the result of circumstances, sometimes of laws, oftener still of these two causes united; but when once established, it may justly be considered as itself the source of almost all the laws, the usages, and the ideas which regulate the conduct of nations: whatever it does not produce, it modifies."[39]

We should judge a society by the character of the people it produces. But we are reluctant to approach a political question from that direction. The reluctance is a reflex of modernity, and it is especially visible in the most vigorously debated sphere of law, that concerning free speech. Justice John Harlan, for example, said that freedom of speech exists "in the hope that use of such freedom will ultimately produce a more capable citizenry and more perfect polity."[40] Notice that however delicately you express the theory—expressing only "hope," not even expectation; and expressing a hope to be realized only "ultimately"—the theory still must link the freedom defended to certain anticipatable, observable, practical results. Furthermore, it must be possible in theory, and should happen in fact, that from time to time there will be occasions when no reasonable person will "hope" that even "ultimately" a particular exercise of free speech—say, racist agitation, or pornography—will contribute to a "more capable citizenry and more perfect polity."

In politics, prudence is always related to probability. But this nation, which began in the modern manner, taking its bearing from the passions, has put aside such calculations or probabilities. It has become a nation wedded to the liberal assumption that the way to deal with passions is to "express" them, to maximize "self-expression." The nation began with the hope that economic self-interestedness would tame a passionate people. And two hundred years later, all of the nation's life is marked by excess, and by disdain for what once was—believe it or not—thought to be a virtue: self-denial. Liberalism, which began as a doctrine for liberating economic egoism, has been hard to confine. It has become a general doctrine of "liberation," which has produced extraordinary abuse of the First Amendment. Even more injurious than the flood of obscenity that has been let loose have been the arguments for letting it loose. One argument is that the concept of "obscenity" is too subjective a category for other than capricious use in law. So *Hustler* magazine must be protected or else *Ulysses* cannot be protected. That is, censorship of anything endangers everything because all standards are equally subjective and idiosyncratic. And consequently, the worth of any act of self-expression is measured not by the worth of what is expressed, but by the benefit to the person who does the expressing. The libertarian position was expressed by former Justice William O. Douglas, who argued on the one hand that censorship is wrong because the premise of a free society is that "people are mature enough to recognize trash" and on the other hand that censorship is wrong because all standards, such as those which distinguish art from trash, are a matter of taste and hence nonrational. Not surprisingly, the New York Civil Liberties Union, which is attuned to the *Zeitgeist*, has said the First Amendment protection of speech means that the state cannot prohibit tattooing, because—all standards being merely subjective—tattooing is an "art form" of equal dignity with any other.

The recent lowering of academic standards reflects, in part,

the same collapse of confidence in standards, and the same celebration of self-expression as a self-justifying process of "liberation." Thus it is considered "elitist," and hence disreputable, to
think that some achievements, and hence some achievers, are
better than others. Anti-elitism is the natural consequence of
liberalism that celebrates "liberation" through "self-expression"
of a spontaneously formed "self." Given this idea, education is
less a matter of putting something into people than of letting
something out of them. That something can be let out only by
"liberation" of the individual from his own inhibitions, and
from society's standards, which are externally "imposed" and
hence repressive. The transformation of the word "elite" into
an epithet is a symptom that society no longer understands that
the political question is always which elites shall rule, not
whether elites shall rule. The use of "elite" as an epithet is
symptomatic of a society in which standards of excellence are
regarded as a form of aggression, an offense against the egalitarian principle that all desires are created equal in moral worth.
At a time when society needs all the excellence and discipline
it can muster, the idea of excellence is regarded as faintly
illiberal, and discipline is regarded as an unjustifiable impediment to spontaneity. The novelist Peter De Vries was carica-
turing such liberalism when he wrote of a girl "who sometimes
spelled the same word two different ways in the same paragraph, thereby showing spontaneity."

It is time for a conservative counterattack, in law and culture
and elsewhere, in the name of those forms of excellence which,
as the Founders said, a free society especially presupposes.
Man, said Aristotle, "is the best of all animals when perfected,
[so] he is the worst of all when sundered from law and justice . . . [because] man is born possessing weapons for the use
of wisdom and virtue, which it is possible to employ entirely
for the opposite ends."[41] Proper conservatism holds that men
and women are biological facts, but that ladies and gentlemen

fit for self-government are social artifacts, creations of the law. The focus of popular government is on the people shaping the law. But remember what Socrates said, in *Crito*, when friends came offering to help him escape the death penalty imposed by Athens. "Are we not first of all your parents?" the laws of Athens ask Socrates, in his imagination, as his friends urge him to flee. "Through us your father took your mother and brought you into the world." Through us you were married and educated, and so "you are our child." That is why George Santayana called patriotism a form of piety, which "may be said to mean man's reverent attachment to the sources of his being and the steadying of his life by that attachment."[42]

Some persons who stop well short of D. H. Lawrence's enthusiasm for the "possibilities of chaos" nevertheless believe that society's thick web of customs and mores is something that grown-up people, or grown-up polities, can put away with other childish things. They feel (in words Learned Hand quoted approvingly) that "convention is like the shell to the chick, a protection till he is strong enough to break it through."[43] But no person or society is ever so "grown-up." Citizens are regulated by a blend of internal and external restraints. The restraining strength of individual habits and social conventions must be inversely proportional to the strength of restraints enforced by law. In the best of times, there is a high ratio of the former to the latter. In the worst of times, "All the decent drapery of life is to be rudely torn off. All the superadded ideas, furnished from the wardrobe of a moral imagination, which the heart owns and the understanding ratifies as necessary to cover the defects of our naked, shivering nature, and to raise it to dignity in our own estimation, are to be exploded as ridiculous, absurd, and antiquated fashion."[44] And "power, of some kind or other, will survive the shock in which manners and opinions perish; and it will find other and worse means for its support."[45]

American politics is currently afflicted by kinds of grim moralizing groups that are coarse in their conceptions, vulgar in analysis and intemperate in advocacy. But the desirable alternative to such groups is not less preoccupation with the sort of questions that interest those groups, but better preoccupation. We need better preoccupation with the legitimate political question of what public actions can do to sustain useful manners and opinions and the rest of "the decent drapery of life." I am not postulating a "reverse Gresham's law" of moral argument; I am not suggesting the soothing thought that good moral arguments will necessarily drive out bad. But I am certain of this: Absent good moral argument, bad moral argument will have the field to itself. People should and will find political ways for venting their moral dimension, and for raising the perennial questions about how we ought to live. People who assert that values are incommensurable are people who have no place in politics, because politics is the business of weighing values against one another and preferring some to others. As Learned Hand said, "There is no democracy among human values, however each may cry out for an equal vote."[46]

No reasonable society wants to erase the distinction between the question "How should man live?" and the question "What behavior should be mandatory?" But it is impossible rationally to stipulate *a priori* limits to the sweep of the law in matters of morality. Such limits must be set by prudential, not theoretical, reasoning. This does not mean that policy shall be unprincipled. It means that its principles must be derived from a sense of national purpose and from evidence as to how law can contribute to the fulfillment of those purposes. So, where does one draw the line? I do not know. Is the drawing of lines potentially dangerous? Yes, indeed. But it is less dangerous than not drawing them. Besides, as Woodrow Wilson, one of the great centralizers of American governmental power, argued, the clearest principle of representative government is that "somebody must be trusted."

All politics takes place on a slippery slope. The most important four words in politics are "up to a point." Are we in favor of free speech? Of course—up to a point. Are we for liberty, equality, military strength, industrial vigor, environmental protection, traffic safety? Up to a point. (Want a significant reduction of traffic deaths? Then ban left turns. You say that would be going too far? Then you are for improving traffic safety—but only up to a point.) Those four words may seem to lack intellectual rigor or heroic commitment. The words do recall Evelyn Waugh's depiction (in his novel *Scoop*) of relations between an autocratic newspaper publisher and his subordinates. The subordinates could make only two responses to his statements: "Yes" and "Up to a point."

Publisher: "Yokohama is the capital of Japan."

Subordinate: "Up to a point, sir."

But "Up to a point" is one answer to many political questions. Political argument often, perhaps usually, is about degree. It is about the point up to which we want to go in pursuit of a good that may, at some point, conflict with other goods. Thus as Burke said, "Political reason is a computing principle; adding, subtracting, multiplying, and dividing, morally and not metaphysically or mathematically, true moral denominations."[47] There is only one political good that we should not speak of wanting only "up to a point." It is the central political value, justice. But then, justice consists of pursuing other political values—such as freedom and virtue—only up to appropriate points.

When law becomes conscious of itself in the sphere of morality, it must also be conscious of the fact that tyranny has frequently been rationalized by a philosophic sleight-of-hand: the insidious assertion that man often wills other than his true

interests, and no one is "really" coerced when he is made to
conform to his true interests, even when he does not recognize
them. The idea that power exercised in the service of virtue is
experienced as something other than power will not convince
those who are on the receiving end of the power. But what is
at issue is not coercion; it is not compelling persons to act
against their settled convictions; it is not a collision of wills, the
state's and the citizen's. Rather, it is a slow, steady, gentle, edu-
cative and persuasive enterprise. Its aim is to dispose citizens
toward certain habits, mores and values, and to increase the
probability that persons will choose to will certain things.

Liberal, bourgeois, democratic—in a word, Lockean—societies
have more complex prerequisites than they seem to think. The
task of making persons competent for life in an open society,
where government rests lightly on society, is a political task
requiring measured involvement of government in encouraging
temperateness, farsightedness and civic spirit. The aim is not
to make society inhospitable to pluralism, but to make pluralism
safe for society. Parents submit the rising generation to compulsory education and other disciplining and enlarging exercises
so that the children shall become adults in more than just
physiological features. A young body matures without much
social intervention; not so a young soul. The body politic re-
produces itself, biologically, just by doing what comes naturally: there is always a rising generation. But the continuance
of the citizenry's moral profile is a matter of political choice.

To say that statecraft is soulcraft is not to say that government should be incandescent with ardor for excellence in everyone and everything at all times. That would be tiresome. Statecraft as soulcraft should mean only a steady inclination,
generally unfelt and unthought. It should mean a disposition,
in the weighing of political persons and measures, to include
consideration of whether they accord with worthy ends for
the polity. Such ends conduce—that word is strong enough—to

the improvement of persons. When this political inclination is a community instinct, there is no question of a particular arm or agency of government's being restlessly responsible for civic virtue. A particular institution charged with the routinized planning of virtue, the way the Federal Highway Administration plans highways, would be ominous and would deserve the ridicule it would receive. A polity which understands that statecraft is soulcraft is not a polity with a distinctive branch grafted on to the trunk of government. It is a polity not with a particular institutional framework, but with a particular frame of mind.

Although something calling itself conservatism has become known for its hostility to government, the hostility only underscores this conservatism's kinship with liberalism. The Western liberal tradition, beginning with Hobbes, has asserted that the essence of the state is coercion. Hobbes asserted a radical disjunction between man utterly free (and constantly anxious) in a state of nature and man seeking safety by surrendering substantial freedom to the state, which Hobbes viewed as primarily an instrument of coercion. Locke postulated civil society antecedent to the state, and therefore could paint a gentler picture of the state's function. But Locke's tints do not alter the essential congruence of his philosophy and Hobbes's. In Locke's scheme of things, rational people join together to invest power in government because society needs government to exercise a monopoly on coercion.

But it is a *non sequitur* to say that because the state has a monopoly on legitimate coercion, its essence is coercion, actual or latent. Proper conservatives proclaim, as Burke did, the gentling function of government. Proper conservatism teaches that authority does not form on high, in the clouds, and clatter down, painfully, like Kansas hailstones. Rather, conservatism teaches that authority grows organically from the rich loam of social mores and structures. A legitimate state—a state with authority, as opposed to a merely authoritarian state—is rooted in such loam.

Only a military government of an occupied city is primarily an instrument of coercion, concerned solely with obedience. The best government exists to frame arrangements in order that they may, over time, become matters of trust. The gradual enlargement of the realm of social trust does not presage the withering away of the state. But it does conduce to an increasingly comfortable fit between institutions and the public, which, like a flowing river, is both a shaper of and shaped by the institutional "banks" between which it flows. A river does not chafe against its banks, except in flood, when it is deformed by unnatural forces. Indeed, a river without banks is incomprehensible; it is a contradiction in terms; it is a lake or a swamp. A river is made by, defined by whatever keeps it to its course.

CHAPTER FIVE

The Broken Chain

> *The effect of liberty to individuals is, that*
> *they may do what they please; we ought*
> *to see what it will please them to do, before*
> *we risk congratulations.*
>
> —EDMUND BURKE

PORTRAITS of America as the confident, unworried "happy republic" have never been entirely accurate. The dour Puritans who started it all had bleak views about man's limitations as a social creature. The Founding Fathers, from Jefferson through Adams, committed treason and waged war, and came away with a melancholy understanding that practical idealism involves the sacrifice of some ideals. Pre–Civil War America was uneasily aware that the yeoman's republic was a vanishing ideal, and post–Civil War America faced industrialization and urbanization with the painfully fresh knowledge that worthy social objectives may require suffering on a large scale. With the late nineteenth century came populism founded on the suspicion that the mass of Americans were exploited by "interests." Then came the progressives, with their political historians proclaiming that the thralldom of the masses was the result of the sly Founders who had drafted an antidemocratic constitution. Pessimism is as American as apple pie—frozen apple pie with a slice of processed cheese.

97

Of the original American immigrants, the Puritans who settled among the chill and damp and rocks of New England, Daniel Boorstin has written, "Never was a people more sure it was on the right track."[1] But, as Boorstin also says, "America began as a sobering experience."[2] The gap between ideals and actualities, between dreams and achievements, the gap that can spur strong men to increased exertions, but can break the spirit of others—this gap is the most conspicuous, continuous landmark in American history. It is conspicuous and continuous not because Americans achieve little, but because they dream grandly. The gap is a standing reproach to Americans; but it marks them off as a special and singularly admirable community among the world's peoples. Americans are overreachers; overreaching is the most admirable and most American of the many American excesses. But in the first half of the nineteenth century, many Americans felt they were reaching for the wrong star.

Before and since, there have been episodes of anxiety that something—some sphere of life, perhaps the citizenry itself—was getting out of control, and taking on a pace and style of life, and a dimension of character, that was unworthy of citizens of a city on a hill. A vague fear of the future was abroad in the land long before Henry Adams "found himself lying in the Gallery of Machines at the Great Exposition of 1900, his historical neck broken by the sudden irruption of forces totally new."[3] As Adams himself dryly noted, "The year 1900 was not the first to upset schoolmasters."[4] Schoolmasters, poets, novelists, politicians, farmers, bankers—Americans from every walk of life—shared a democratically distributed worry in the second quarter of the nineteenth century. They were feeling a little queasy as a result of hard choices posed by American possibilities. The uneasiness is in evidence in the writings of Emerson and Thoreau. It is in some of James Fenimore Cooper's novels, most brilliantly in *Home as Found*. The words of two eminent

Americans make manifest the change in the American temper.

In 1783, at the end of the Revolutionary upheaval and in the period before the Constitutional Convention, Americans were living under the Articles of Confederation and were enduring what some historians call "the critical period" of American history. Perhaps it was a dangerous era. But the preeminent American was not weighed down by the cares of the day. In 1783, George Washington said:

> The foundation of our Empire was not laid in the gloomy age of Ignorance and Superstition, but at an Epoch when the rights of mankind were better understood and more clearly defined, than at any former period, the researches of the human mind, after social happiness, have been carried to a great extent, the Treasures of knowledge, acquired by the labours of Philosophers, Sages and Legislatures, through a long succession of years, are laid open for our use, and their collected wisdom may be happily applied in the Establishment of our forms of Government; . . . At this auspicious period, the United States came into existence as a Nation, and if their Citizens should not be completely free and happy, the fault will be intirely their own.[5]

Seventy years later, another great but very different American was voicing anxieties about a nation that was much more than seventy years older in spirit. In 1852 Emerson made this entry in his journals:

> The head of Washington hangs in my dining-room for a few days past, and I cannot keep my eyes off of it. It has a certain Appalachian strength, as if it were truly the first-fruits of America, and expressed the Country. The heavy, leaden eyes turn on you, as the eyes of an ox in a pasture. And the mouth has a gravity and depth of quiet, as if this Man had absorbed all the serenity of America, and left none for his restless, rickety, hysterical countrymen.[6]

The America of 1852 was older and wiser and, in some ways, sadder than Washington's America. But in another sense, the America of 1852 was younger than Washington's America.

The America of 1783 had just finished shaking off a robust and overbearing mother country. That America was the product of the brisk evolution of different but related colonies into a larger community of shared values and interests. That America was at least partially unified by the common endeavor of rebellion in defense of traditional rights. The Americans of 1783 were not an old people in the scheme of world history, but they were a people, and they could feel their roots secure in a moving, changing but continuous tradition. They could look to the future as a realm of promise. It promised more rapid change, but in 1783 change was the American way, and change was considered a process of unalloyed promise.

By 1852, many Americans looked at things differently. They were worried about the future, and not only because an irrepressible conflict over slavery was upon them. Americans in 1852 worried about the future because they sensed an ominous gap between themselves and the founding era. They were being transformed by the dynamic of American life.

Many American agreements, arguments and aspirations, like America's institutions, show a remarkable continuity. Yet this continuous American citizenry—this national "person"—is a "twice-born" person. A rural, agricultural and federated nation has become an urban, industrial and consolidated nation, and has found being "twice born" rather unnerving. Americans prized their initial birth as a rural yeomen's republic. It seemed heroic and immaculate. Hence they were not uniformly and unambiguously enthusiastic about being reborn. The second quarter of the nineteenth century was an era of American ambivalence about being "reborn."

Being born is a rude and shocking experience. We all come barging into life in an ungraceful and involuntary manner.

That is probably good, because it sets a useful and sober tone for life. Frank Skeffington, protagonist in *The Last Hurrah*, said that man's best friend is the compromise. From birth on, life is a series of compromises with the world. But nations can fret and reflect and even resist when confronted with the prospect of being reborn. When Americans were faced with compromising their cherished self-image as a virtuous yeomen's republic, they balked. They felt confronted with an agonizing choice. Against the receding vision of yeoman's simplicity stood the prospect of a sophisticated modern nation dedicated to applied enlightenment, a nation of power, wealth, comfort and progress. The clashing visions represented round two of the Jefferson–Hamilton argument about the nature and destiny of the American nation. This time, the lure of Hamiltonian dreams combined with the impetus of America's natural endowments to carry the day. America was gearing up for growth and was coming face to face with this question: What marks will the enthusiastic pursuit of growth, power, wealth and progress leave on the character of the nation, and the characters of the citizens? De Tocqueville, who was here at the time, wrote:

> I am aware that many of my contemporaries maintain that nations are never their own masters here below, and that they necessarily obey some insurmountable and unintelligent power, arising from anterior events, from their race, or from the soil and climate of their country. Such principles are false and cowardly; such principles can never produce aught but feeble men and pusillanimous nations. Providence has not created mankind entirely independent or entirely free. It is true that around every man a fatal circle is traced beyond which he cannot pass; but within the wide verge of that circle he is powerful and free; as it is with man, so with communities.[7]

The question, then as now, was this: Will diverse and even noble characters flourish in a society in which the political order takes its bearings from the low but predictable passions of men?

Americans have always had Emersons to remind them that money represents "the prose of life." They have sometimes been reluctant to consider whether there is anything but prose in life; or whether there is a poetry of life which they are missing as a people; or whether the nation's political practices so singlemindedly facilitate the pursuit of the prose of life that they ignore the poetry. This view, along with familiar forebodings, was voiced by Henry Adams in his great history of the Jefferson and Madison administrations. At the end of the final volume of that history Adams wrote:

> In 1815 for the first time Americans ceased to doubt the path they were to follow. . . . American character was formed, if not fixed. . . . American types were especially worth study if they were to represent the greatest democratic evolution the world could know. . . . That the individual should rise to a higher order either of intelligence or morality than had existed in former ages was not to be expected, for the United States offered less field for the development of individuality than had been offered by older and smaller societies. The chief function of the American Union was to raise the average standard of popular intelligence and well-being, and at the close of the War of 1812 the superior average intelligence of Americans was so far admitted that the Yankee acuteness, or smartness, became a national reproach; but much doubt remained whether the intelligence belonged to a high order, or proved a high morality. From the earliest ages, shrewdness was associated with unscrupulousness; and Americans were freely charged with wanting honesty. The charge could neither be proved nor disproved. American morality was such as suited a people so endowed, and was high when compared with the morality of many older societies but, like American intelligence, it discouraged excess.

. . . Like the character of the popular inventions, the character of the morals corresponded to a growing democratic society; but time alone could decide whether it would result in a high or low national ideal."[8]

Perhaps the national ideal was settled much earlier by the national acceptance of a liberal political order. But that does not alter the fact that in the first half of the nineteenth century many Americans became aware of, and uneasy about, their destiny. This anxiety was anticipated in the debate between Jefferson and Hamilton. Jefferson, surprisingly, was Henry Adams' precursor. Although commonly considered the most optimistic of the Founders, Jefferson was among the most pessimistic. Or, more precisely, his thinking contained the largest scope for anxiety about the future, and especially about the future that in fact came to pass. As Richard Hofstadter said:

Certainly the balance of Jefferson's good society is a tenuous thing: the working class is corrupt; merchants are corrupt; speculators are corrupt; cities are "pestilential"; only farmers are dependably good. Sunder human nature from its proper or "natural" nourishment in the cultivation of the soil and the ownership of real property, and he profoundly distrusts it. Sunder democracy from the farm and how much more firmly does he believe in it than John Adams?[9]

Jefferson's sketch of the good society is justly famous:

Those who labor in the earth are the chosen people of God, if ever He had a chosen people, whose breasts He has made His peculiar deposit for substantial and genuine virtue. It is the focus in which he keeps alive that sacred fire, which otherwise might escape from the face of the earth. Corruption of morals in the mass of cultivators is a phenomenon of which no age nor nation has furnished an example. It is the mark set on those, who, not looking up to heaven, to their own soil and industry, as does the husbandman, for their subsistence, depend for it on casualties and caprice of customers. Dependence begets subservience and venality, suffocates the germ of virtue, and prepares fit tools for the designs of ambition. This, the natural progress and consequence of the arts, has sometimes perhaps been retarded by accidental circumstances; but, generally speaking, the proportion which the aggregate of the other classes of citizens bears in any State to that of its husbandmen, is the proportion of its unsound to its healthy parts . . . While we have land to labor then, let us never wish to see our citizens occupied at a workbench, or twirling a distaff . . . for the general operations of manufacture, let our workshops remain in Europe.[10]

But events do not always deal gently with one's preferences, even if one is Jefferson. War is the shaping force of the modern world, and it helped undo Jefferson's world. In 1814 he wrote: "Our enemy has indeed the consolation of Satan on removing our first parents from Paradise: from a peaceable and agricultural nation, he makes us a military and manufacturing one."[11] The year before, Jefferson, suddenly a manufacturer, had written:

I have hitherto myself depended entirely on foreign manufactures; but I have now thirty-five spindles agoing, a hand carding machine, and looms with the flying shuttle, for the supply of my own farms. The continuance of the war will fix the habit generally, and out of the evils of impressment and of the orders of council a great blessing for us will grow. I have not formerly been an advocate for great manufactories. I doubted whether our labor, employed in agriculture, and aided by the spontaneous energies of the earth, would not procure us more than we could make ourselves of other necessities. But other considerations entering into the question, have settled my doubts.[12]

Et tu, Tom? Actually, the die had been cast years before. On July 4—a resonant date—1789, the year the Constitution was ratified, Congress put customs duties on all imports. Two weeks later it placed much higher tonnage duties on foreign vessels than on American vessels. Clearly Congress, like the country, was determined that there were going to be lots of workshops in America. In his "Report on Public Credit," submitted to Congress January 14, 1790, Hamilton proposed funding the entire national debt (about $55 million) at face value, plus unpaid interest, in spite of the fact that speculators had bought up most of the debt from soldiers and others who had lost faith in the nation's ability or willingness to pay. Hamilton's program may have been enacted because many Congressmen were speculators. But his plan derived from an idea, a vision of a particular kind of America—and American.

It is, of course, rare that a nation has a moment of decision in which it can be said to choose an economic system. But the United States had such a moment, albeit a moment extending over four decades. It involved healthily moralistic political debate.

In the twentieth century we seem to have lost the knack—or taste—for defining our policy choices with reference to philosophic fundamentals. We have committed taxidermy on moral categories, draining them of their richness and stuffing them full of sawdust talk of "rights" and "interests" and interstate commerce. But there was a vigorous moral definition of a social choice in the debate between Jeffersonians and Hamiltonians. The debate came to a kind of culmination in the Jacksonian-era controversy about the national bank. It was a debate about the coming of industrial capitalism, and pessimism, to America.

Who won the fight for the American future? The author of the sentiment "Let our workshops remain in Europe"? Or the author of the "Report on Manufacture," with its call for institutions of credit to fuel industrialization? Looking back from 1839 at the "great and visible economic improvement occurring around 1790," John Marshall wrote that "the influence of the Constitution on habits of thinking and acting, though silent, was considerable."[13] Marshall's pioneering contribution, judicial review, may or may not have been a constitutional afterthought improvised by him. Certainly it was, initially, an instrument for protecting, against the excesses of state legislatures, the supremacy of the national market. It was used to guarantee the prerequisites of a commercial republic—the sort of republic assumed by the liberal democratic theory underlying the Constitution. Judicial review may have been an afterthought, but it served the original and primary thought. Both the thought and the afterthought were pregnant with the Hamiltonian future.

Woodrow Wilson called Hamilton "a great man, but not a great American." Today in the Federal City—the seat of the government that Hamilton did more than anyone except Washington to establish—there is a splendid memorial to Hamilton's rival, Jefferson. There is no Hamilton memorial. But if you seek his monument, look around. This is Hamilton's America. Even agriculture is a heavily mechanized and science-intensive industry. In fact, this was Hamilton's country by the time the Jacksonians, fighting a rearguard Jeffersonian action against history, opposed that "monster," the national bank.

Andrew Jackson said that planters (he was a planter), farmers, mechanics and laborers are "the bone and sinew of the country." By implication, everyone else is part of the fat. The crucial matter was not amounts of wealth (Jackson was a wealthy planter). Rather, it was the methods of acquisition. The assumption was that different methods produced distinguishing character traits and moral orientations. In Martin Van Buren's formulation, persons who live honorably "by the sweat of their brow" are superior to those who live nimbly "by their wits." (It is a recurring theme: "His name was George F. Babbitt. He was forty-six years old now, in April, 1920, and he made nothing in particular, neither butter nor shoes nor poetry, but he was nimble in the calling of selling houses for more than people could afford to pay.")[14]

Madison, too, focused less on the ownership of property than on the production of it. Government exists to protect process more than possession—the process of acquisition. In all that the Founding Fathers wrote about property, there is almost no hint of the aristocratic doctrine of property. The aristocratic doctrine is that property is the ground of leisure, elevated sentiments and noble pursuits, including liberality toward those who are less adept or less fortunate regarding property. The Founding Fathers' doctrine of property is a doctrine for and about the masses. It is a doctrine for taming the many, not for elevating the few. Different doctrines of property are apt to have practical consequences. For example, an aristocratic view of property is apt to suggest policies permitting the transmission of property intact through inheritance, the better to foster the formation of large-spirited families. A democratic view of property is more consistent with—some say it entails—severe, even confiscatory, inheritance taxes to prevent large and stable accumulations, which make the process of acquisition less general and wholesomely tumultuous than it otherwise would be.

The Jacksonians believed that enterprise is a toughening, purging, restoring tonic for the Republic if—but only if—it occurs without large-scale credit mechanisms. Abundant credit creates the requisite liquidity for rapid growth and social dynamism, but the inevitable concomitant of all that is "speculators." Fifty years ago some "progressives" believed that a Keynesian state, administered by educated bureaucrats ("an elite of unassuming experts" was Beatrice Webb's oxymoron), could use democratic political institutions to allocate capital and dispense with the capitalist class. One hundred and fifty years ago the Jacksonians understood that capitalism must be driven by "new men," those "speculators," served by the national bank, who would set a new tone for the nation. Hear the

anguished cry of William Leggett, a Jacksonian anticipating
the loss of a Jeffersonian society:

> Take a hundred ploughmen promiscuously from their
> fields, and a hundred merchants from their desks, and what
> man, regarding the true dignity of his nature, could hesitate
> to give the award of superior excellence, in every main in-
> tellectual, physical, and moral respect, to the band of
> hardy rustics, over that of the lank, and sallow accoun-
> tants, worn out with the sordid anxieties of traffic and the
> calculations of gain? Yet the merchant shall grow rich
> from participation in the unequal privileges which a false
> system of legislation has created, while the ploughman, un-
> protected by the laws, and dependent wholly on himself,
> shall barely earn a frugal livelihood by continued toil.[15]

The vigor of Jacksonian debate was commensurate with the
felt stakes of the argument, which was about the kind of people
Americans ought to plan to be. I say "plan" because they felt
they had foresight, and a choice. Actually, they did not have
much choice.

To the extent that the Puritans carried the germ of philosophic modernity in their politics, De Tocqueville correctly
said that the "destiny of America was embodied in the first
Puritan who landed on those shores."[16] When Jefferson was
worrying about people being "piled up in cities" (1782), Boston had a population about equal to that of Muskogee, Okla-
homa, today. In 1790, fewer than 4 percent of Americans lived
in towns with more than 8,000 inhabitants. At the time (1821)
that a Jeffersonian was warning, colorfully, of "the ring of
streaked and speckled population of our large towns and cities,"
there were only twelve cities with even 10,000 inhabitants,
speckled or otherwise. The nineteenth century, a century of
railroads and hence of railheads, gave the world Chicago. It also
was the century of those who built the railroads—the immigrants. They passed through Hell's Kitchen, en route to Levit-

town. But they always were building Hamilton's America.

The nineteenth century was not the first era alive to the connection between particular economic institutions and particular human types. But it was especially alive. "The hand-mill gives you society with the feudal lord; the steam-mill, society with the industrial capitalist," wrote Marx.[17] Marx believed that technological change is the engine of history. He was complacent about that because he believed that history is necessarily progressive. Jefferson, not being a historicist, was denied that consolation. Long before Marx and Darwin argued that as creatures act upon the world, they act upon themselves, Jefferson insisted that modes of production shape the producers. He understood that history is the history of the mind. He thought that American democracy depended on Americans of an appropriate character—the independent character of rural yeomen. Hence, American democracy required "an immensity of land." So when the opportunity arose for the Louisiana Purchase, he leaped at it, kicking over the traces of his strict construction of the Constitution's allocation of executive powers. His sociological analysis of the needs of republicanism took precedence over his institutional analysis of Constitutional niceties.

De Tocqueville, the foremost student of the social roots of character in a commercial republic, was a traveler with a mission. He wanted to discover the causes that were giving rise to the American as a social type. And he wanted to decide whether a commercial republic tends, inherently, to better humanity:

> We must first understand what is wanted of society and its government. Do you wish to give a certain elevation to the human mind and teach it to regard the things of this world with generous feelings, to inspire men with a scorn of mere temporal advantages, to form and nourish strong convictions and keep alive the spirit of honorable devoted-

ness? Is it your object to refine the habits, embellish the manners, and cultivate the arts, to promote the love of poetry, beauty and glory? Would you constitute a people fitted to act powerfully upon all other nations, and prepared for those high enterprises which, whatever be their results, will leave a name forever famous in history? If you believe such to be the principal object of society, avoid the government of the democracy, for it would not lead you with certainty to the goal.

But if you hold it expedient to divert the moral and intellectual activity of man to the production of comfort and the promotion of general well-being; if a clear understanding be more profitable to man than genius; if your object is not to stimulate the virtues of heroism, but the habits of peace; if you had rather witness vices than crimes, and are content to meet with fewer noble deeds, provided offenses be diminished in the same proportion; if, instead of living in the midst of a brilliant society, you are contented to have prosperity around you; if, in short, you are of the opinion that the principal object of a government is not to confer the greatest possible power and glory upon the body of the nation, but to ensure the greatest enjoyment and to avoid the most misery to each of the individuals who compose it—if such be your desire, then equalize the conditions of men and establish democratic institutions.[18]

Yes, we must first understand what national character we want government to foster, because all else follows. Two things surprised De Tocqueville in America, "the mutability of the greater part of human actions, and the singular stability of certain principles. Men are in constant motion; the mind of man appears almost unmoved."[19] There is little time for mind when there is so much of motion:

In the United States a man builds a house in which to spend his old age, and he sells it before the roof is on; he

plants a garden and lets it just as the trees are coming into
bearing; he brings a field into tillage and leaves other men
to gather the crops; he embraces a profession and gives it
up; he settles in a place, which he soon afterward leaves
to carry his changeable longings elsewhere. If his private
affairs leave him any leisure, he instantly plunges into the
vortex of politics; and if at the end of a year of unremit-
ting labor he finds he has a few days' vacation, his eager
curiosity whirls him over the vast extent of the United
States, and he will travel fifteen hundred miles in a few
days to shake off his happiness. Death at length overtakes
him, but it is before he is weary of his bootless chase of
that complete felicity which forever escapes him.[20]

Obviously that is overdrawn, or else the Warren Court
would have declared American life unconstitutional (as a vio-
lation of the proscription of "cruel and unusual punishments").
But there is truth in De Tocqueville's picture of anxious, even
gloomy hedonism. He foresaw a new "species of oppression"
imposed by a powerful government using its power narrowly
but energetically for the material comfort of the citizenry. And
he worried about the citizenry's becoming "a flock of timid
and industrious animals of which government is the shepherd."
The despotism that democracies must fear would be solicitous
toward the citizens, working

to secure their gratifications and to watch over their fate.
That power is absolute, minute, regular, provident, and
mild. It would be like the authority of a parent if, like
that authority, its object was to prepare men for man-
hood; but it seeks, on the contrary, to keep them in perpetual childhood: it is well content that the people should
rejoice, provided they think of nothing but rejoicing.
For their happiness such a government willingly labors,
but it chooses to be the sole agent and the only arbiter of
that happiness; it provides for their security, foresees and
supplies their necessities, facilitates their pleasures, man-

ages their principal concerns, directs their industry, regulates the descent of property, and subdivides their inheritances: what remains, but to spare them all the care of thinking and all the trouble of living? . . . The will of man is not shattered, but softened, bent, and guided.[21]

The telltale word is "mild." Such government is mild in order to make men soft and mild. This condition was discerned approvingly by another traveler French by birth, fifty years before De Tocqueville. In his *Letters from an American Farmer* (1782), J. Hector St. John Crèvecoeur describes with approving wonder how "the various Christian sects . . . wear out, and how religious indifference becomes prevalent"[22] in America. Crèvecoeur set out to describe Pennsylvania, not to illustrate the animating value and dynamic of a liberal society. But he did both in a passage that has the power of a naive painting:

When any considerable number of a particular sect happen to dwell contiguous to each other, they immediately erect a temple, and there worship the Divinity agreeably to their own peculiar ideas. Nobody disturbs them. If any new sect springs up in Europe, it may happen that many of its professors will come and settle in America. As they bring their zeal with them, they are at liberty to make proselytes if they can, and to build a meeting and to follow the dictates of their consciences; for neither the government nor any other power interferes. If they are peaceable subjects, and are industrious, what is it to their neighbours how and in what manner they think fit to address their prayers to the Supreme Being? But if the sectaries are not settled close together, if they are mixed with other denominations, their zeal will cool for want of fuel, and will be extinguished in a little time. Then the Americans become as to religion, what they are as to country, allied to all. In them the name of Englishman, Frenchman, and European is lost, and in like manner, the strict modes of Christianity as practised in Europe are lost also. This effect will extend itself still farther hereafter, and though this may appear to you as a strange idea, yet it is a very true one. . . .

Let us suppose you and I to be travelling; we observe that in this house, to the right, lives a Catholic, who prays to God as he has been taught, and believes in transubstantiation; he works and raises wheat, he has a large family of children, all hale and robust; his belief, his prayers offend nobody. About one mile farther on the same road, his next neighbour may be a good honest plodding German Lutheran, who addresses himself to the same God, the God of all, agreeably to the modes he has been educated in, and believes in consubstantiation; by so doing he scandalizes nobody; he also works in his fields, embellishes the earth, clears swamps, &c. What has the world to do with his Lutheran principles? He persecutes nobody, and nobody persecutes him, he visits his neighbours, and his neighbours visit him. Next to him lives a seceder, the most enthusiastic of all sectaries; his zeal is hot and fiery, but separated as he is from others of the same complexion, he has no congregation of his own to resort to, where he might cabal and mingle religious pride with worldly obstinacy. He likewise raises good crops, his house is handsomely painted, his orchard is one of the fairest in the neighbourhood. How does it concern the welfare of the country, or of the province at large, what this man's religious sentiments are, or really whether he has any at all? He is a good farmer, he is a sober, peaceable, good citizen: William Penn himself would not wish for more. This is the visible character; the invisible one is only guessed at, and is nobody's business. Next again lives a Low Dutchman, who implicitly believes the rules laid down by the synod of Dort. He conceives no other idea of a clergyman than that of an hired man; if he does his work well he will pay him the stipulated sum; if not he will dismiss him, and do without sermons, and let his church be shut up for years. But notwithstanding this coarse idea, you will find his house and farm to be the neatest in all the country; and you will judge by his waggon and fat horses, that he thinks more of the affairs of this world than of those of the next. He is sober and laborious, therefore he is all he ought to be as to the affairs of this life; as for those of the next, he must trust to the great Creator. Each of these people instruct their children as well as they can, but these instructions are feeble compared to those which are given to the youth of the poorest class in Europe. Their children will therefore grow up less zealous and more indifferent in matters of religion than their parents. The foolish vanity, or rather the fury, of making Proselytes, is unknown here; they have no time, the seasons call for all their attention, and thus in a few years, this mixed neighbourhood will exhibit a strange religious medley, that will be neither pure Catholicism nor pure Calvinism. A very perceptible indifference even in the first generation, will become apparent; and it may happen that the daughter of the Catholic will marry the son of the seceder, and settle by themselves at a distance from their parents. What religious education will they give their children? A very imperfect one. If there happens to be in the neighbourhood any place of worship, we will suppose a Quaker's meeting; rather than not shew their fine clothes, they will go to it, and some of them may perhaps attach themselves to that society. Others will remain in a perfect state of indifference; the children of these zealous parents will not be able to tell what their religious principles are, and their grandchildren still less. The neighbourhood of a place of worship generally leads them to it, and the action of going thither, is the strongest evidence they can give of their attachment to any sect. . . . Thus all sects are mixed as well as all nations; thus religious indifference is imperceptibly disseminated from one end of the continent to the other; which is at present one of the

strongest characteristics of the Americans. Where this will
reach no one can tell, perhaps it may leave a vacuum fit to
receive other systems. Persecution, religious pride, the love
of contradiction, are the food of what the world commonly calls religion. These motives have ceased here: zeal
in Europe is confined; here it evaporates in the great distance it has to travel; there it is a grain of powder inclosed;
here it burns away in the open air, and consumes without
effect.[23]

Imported religious zeal is tolerable as long as the zealots are
"peaceable" and "industrious," which means as long as there is
economic zeal. Soon religious zeal will cool, and "strict modes"
of religion will disappear. If there must be religion, let it be
lax. In America, belief in transubstantiation is insubstantial and
unimportant compared with solid concerns, such as wheat.
What has the work of the world—clearing swamps, and so
forth—to do with consubstantiation or Lutheran principles? No
religious principle concerns "the welfare of the country," because that welfare is a material matter. It involves neat houses,
fat horses, fine wagons and other concerns of people "who
think more of the affairs of this world than of those of the
next." Best of all, the religious instruction of children is inevitably "very imperfect" and "feeble," and the generations
become progressively "indifferent." Tolerance is acceptable
because "mere" opinion is insubstantial when compared with
solid "interests." Tolerance is a blessing because it breeds indifference. Religious impulses are, by nature, hot and volatile.
As they are supplanted by the cooler, solider preoccupations—
the calculations of commerce—the polity will become more
stable.

But a slower pulse in the body politic need not mean stability, or at least not that of a healthy mind. It can mean en-
feeblement and enervation. Crèvecoeur did not seem troubled

by the possibility that as the moral intensity of individuals is lowered, social bonds may be weakened. De Tocqueville was more prescient. Consider his majestic but melancholy anticipation of how Americans would become "undifferentiated":

> Among democratic nations new families are constantly springing up, others are constantly falling away, and all that remain change their condition; the woof of time is every instant broken and the track of generations effaced. Those who went before are soon forgotten; of those who will come after, no one has any idea: the interest of man is confined to those in close propinquity to himself. As each class gradually approaches others and mingles with them, its members become undifferentiated and lose their class identity for each other. Aristocracy had made a chain of all members of the community, from the peasant to the king; democracy breaks that chain and severs every link of it . . .
>
> Thus not only does democracy make every man forget his ancestors, but it hides his descendants and separates his contemporaries from him; it throws him back forever upon himself alone and threatens in the end to confine him entirely within the solitude of his own heart.[24]

When De Tocqueville wrote about the "interests" of citizens in a commercial republic being steadily narrowed, about "the track of generations effaced," about ancestors forgotten, about the chain of community being broken, it was 1832. Just a generation later, Lincoln, struggling against the disintegration of the American community, invoked "the mystic chords of memory":

> Though passion may have strained, it must not break our bonds of affection. The mystic chords of memory, stretching from every battlefield, and patriot grave, to every liv-

ing heart and hearthstone, all over this broad land, will yet swell the chorus of the Union when again touched, as surely they will be, by the better angels of our nature.[25]

The bonds strained by the slavery controversy were, as Crèvecoeur and De Tocqueville understood, made flimsy by the normal day-by-day life of lonely self-interestedness in a commercial republic. Lincoln towers over our national experience because, in the nation's moment of maximum desperation, he marshaled that which makes us human—language—against the notion that "there is no right principle of action but *self-interest*."[26] That notion, which is always toxic, was nearly fatal to the Union in the middle of the nineteenth century. Today, the prevalence of that notion makes the nation vulnerable to internal decay and external challenge.

It is all very well for Americans, encouraged by conservatives, to insist, as the unconservative Tom Paine did, that "formal government makes but a small part of civilised life," and that the "safety and prosperity of the individual" depends far more on "the unceasing circulation of interest, which, passing through its million channels, invigorates the whole mass of civilized man."[27] But is the vigor that derives from the circulation of interests enough to secure the public good? It was not in Lincoln's day, and it is not now.

The lacuna in the political philosophy of modernity is provision for social cohesion. Such provision must involve a degree of nurturing of the shared "national mind." Man's natural aggressiveness, which Hobbes was first to make the central fact of politics, has not been denied by subsequent philosophers of liberal democratic commercial (which is to say, capitalist) societies. Rather, they have argued for the sublimation of this aggressiveness in commerce. To the extent that modern philosophy postulates any sort of natural sociability of mankind, that sociability leads not to political but to commercial relations—

not to the Athenian agora or the Roman forum but to the New York Stock Exchange.

Classical economics and liberal democratic political philosophy arise from the same psychological and epistemological doctrines. That is one reason why, in bourgeois societies, political philosophy has had a tendency to disappear into economics, and economics has striven to become a comprehensive theory of social energy. The shift in the focus of political philosophy, from concern for man's inner life to concern for his behavior and material well-being, has coincided with the rise of the social sciences, and capitalism. That is, the shift has coincided with growing confidence in man's ability to manipulate the natural and social worlds.

The shift has produced a defect in the practice of politics, especially in this, the most modern nation. One way of correcting the defect is with a conservative doctrine of political economy. To some, this will seem a faintly disreputable idea, or perhaps even a contradiction in terms. Today's conservatives are apt to insist that the great virtue of their economic doctrine is that it separates politics and the economy. But if economic policy is not politics—the authoritative assignment of social values—then what is?

Today's conservatives have a remarkably bifurcated view of the world. As a result, they often seem like startled innocents, alarmed at the social consequences of the economic doctrine that serves as their political philosophy, and unaware that "social issues" and "economic policy" are inseparable facets of "the political." It is odd that conservatives, who are custodians of the claims of continuity against the willfulness of the moment, present an economic doctrine as a political philosophy. Economics is about contemporary calculations of short-term interests; it is about the immediate and the quantifiable, to the exclusion of the venerable and sentimental. Socialism is, of

course, an economic doctrine that claims to lead people away
from merely economic calculations. But socialism is an expression of the disease for which it purports to be the cure.
Socialists generally assert the primacy of economic motivations,
the dominance of economic conflict in fueling social change
and the urgency of organizing public action around economic
interests and objectives. The very name of Britain's Labour
Party affirms the propriety, even inevitability of class conflict
as an organizing principle of political action. Although socialism deals with individuals aggregated, it is just another variant
of the liberal democratic tradition, another doctrine of acquisi-
tive individualism.

Economics is a science of individualism; true conservatives
have a soft spot in their hearts for organic collectivity. It is
small wonder that there is no truly conservative economic doctrine. True conservatives think people spend too much time
thinking and acting "economically." (Remember Burke's lament: "But the age of chivalry is gone. That of sophists, econ-
omists, and calculators has succeeded, and the glory of Europe
is extinguished forever.")[28] It is small wonder that in the United
States, which has always encouraged individualism, ambition
and mobility at the expense of stability and community, real
conservatism has been a marginal and primarily cultural school
of criticism.

Having hollowed out their political philosophy to make
room for an economic doctrine—a doctrine that recommends
capitalism for its unsleeping dynamism—contemporary American conservatives are in a singularly weak position to perform
the traditional conservative function of judging and editing the
social transformation that comes with the dissolution of old
forms and modes of action. Traditional conservatism has not
been, and proper conservatism cannot be, merely a defense of
industrialism and individualist "free-market" economics. Con-

servatism is about the cultivation and conservation of certain values, or it is nothing. But industrialism has been a thorough solvent of traditional values, a revolutionary force for change. It is unreasonably *a priori* to assume that the unregulated consequences of unfettered industrialism—whatever they may be— are compatible with, let alone identifiable with, conservative aspirations.

Conservatives rightly defend the market as a marvelous mechanism for allocating resources. But when conservatives begin regarding the market less as an expedient than as an ultimate value, or the ultimate arbiter of all values, their conservatism degenerates into the least conservative political impulse, which is populism. After all, the market is the judgment of "the people" at any moment. But government, especially conservative government, exists not merely to serve individuals' immediate preferences, but to achieve collective purposes for an ongoing nation. Government must take the long view. Government, unlike an economic market, has responsibilities. It has a duty to look down the road and consider the interests and needs of citizens yet unborn. The market has a remarkable ability to satisfy the desires of the day. Government has other, graver purposes.

Today, after two centuries of remarkable conformity of practice to theory—the political philosophy of modernity, and the practices of liberal democracies—the urgent tasks of government include mending and maintaining the "chain of community." In any society scope must be given, and in liberal democratic societies ample scope has been given, to the egoistic motives of ambition and accumulation. The political system must also incorporate altruistic motives. It does so in domestic policies associated with the phrase "welfare state." These are policies that express the community's acceptance of an ethic of common provision. It would be misleading were the term "altruistic" to obscure the practicality of such policies.

Altruism—principled regard for others—is not optional. It is necessary for strengthening the sense of community that the theory and practice of modern politics attenuates. In our time, this strengthening should be a focus of the field of study once known, usefully, as political economy.

CHAPTER SIX

Conservative Political Economy

Protection is not a principle, but an expedient.

—BENJAMIN DISRAELI

IN 1964, a conservative citizen, speaking with the zeal of a convert, which he was, gave a nationally televised speech in support of Barry Goldwater's candidacy. The citizen denounced "people who view the tax as a means of achieving changes in our social structure."[1] In 1981, in another speech, the same fellow said approximately the same thing:

> The taxing power of government must be used to provide revenues for legitimate government purposes. It must not be used to regulate the economy or bring about social change.[2]

Now, the consistency of Ronald Reagan's views is one of the wonders of American political life. But another wonder is that anyone, especially the fortieth President, would talk like that. No previous President has stressed as much as Ronald Reagan has the possibility and importance of changing society by changing the tax code. Clearly, Reagan came to Washington convinced that certain tax changes are the key to his economic program, which is, in turn, the key to his comprehensive plan for revitalizing American society and improving Americans' spirits. He obviously believes that public policies should reward and thereby nurture the attributes essential to strength (industriousness, thrift, deferral of gratification) and should discourage the attributes inimical to economic vitality (idleness, dissipation, self-indulgence). And he would not deny that laws establishing, protecting and regulating the institution of property are examples of kinds of laws that have the effect, intended or not, of shaping the spirit of society. Tax deductions and tax exemptions are not alternatives to social programs. They are social programs. And unlike many such, they often achieve their intended effects. They alter behavior on a large scale for the advancement of chosen goals.

In the 1976 campaign for the Republican presidential nomination, Reagan repeatedly said: "I've always thought that the best thing government can do is nothing." But surely the truth, regarding every significant aspect of social life, is that the one thing government cannot do is "nothing." This is true in two senses. First, a decision not to alter the *status quo* is a decision to do something. It is a decision to continue the public policies— the complex weave of laws and customs—that underlie any significant sphere of social action. Second, it is peculiar to speak as though *laissez-faire* policies amounted to government's "doing nothing." Conservatives rightly cultivate a saving sense of the complexity of the social organism, a sense that protects society from the overbearing political pretense that government can superintend all relationships. But a "free-market" economic system is a system; it is a public product, a creation of government. Any important structure of freedom is a structure, a complicated institutional and cultural context that government must nurture and sustain.

Obviously "free speech" is not free in the sense that it is free of prerequisites; it is not free of a complicated institutional

frame. Free speech, as much as a highway system, is something
government must establish and maintain. The government of
a country without the rare and fragile traditions of civility,
without education and communication capabilities, could proclaim freedom of speech and resolutely stand back. But the result would not be free speech. It would be mayhem, and the
triumph of incivility. Similarly, a capitalistic economic system,
with all the institutions, laws, regulations, dispositions, habits
and skills that make it work, is not part of the constitution of
the universe. It does not spring up from the social soil unbid-
den, like prairie grass. It requires an educational system, bank-
ing and currency systems, highly developed laws of commerce
and much more.

Many conservatives are fond of the epigram that the phrase
"political economy" represents the marriage of two words that
should be divorced on the grounds of incompatibility. But
clear-minded persons can more reasonably object to the phrase
on the ground that the adjective "political" is a superfluous
modifier because any economic arrangement is, by definition,
a political arrangement. Try to define "the political" in a way
that severs it from ideas central to economic life—ownership, contracts, corporations, trade unions, the right to strike,
antitrust principles. Of course, before the Depression nationalized concern with "the economy," the use of the definite
article would have seemed odd. Few people then thought about
the nation's aggregate economic output. Even just sixty years
ago, economic statistics were so rudimentary that the central
government did not know how many people were employed,
or wanted to be, or what the Gross National Product was. It
had no need to know, in the sense that it acknowledged no
clear responsibility for policies that required a sophisticated
national information base. But since late October 1929, the
public has felt bound up with a single economic dynamic, and
this feeling has found consistent expression in a political fact:

The President is held accountable for the aggregate economic performance.

Conservatives are understandably impatient with the familiar liberal formulation about "giving human rights priority over property rights." But conservatives, in their eagerness to put government in its place (which they think is down, and far away), argue just as fatuously that "only people produce wealth; government does not." Government produces the infrastructure of society—legal, physical, educational, from highways through skills—that is a precondition for the production of wealth. The unlovely locution "human capital" reflects the impulse to reduce all social categories to economic ones, but it also reflects a recognition that investment must be made in people before they can be socially competent. And it is obvious, once you think about it, that government is, and must be, a major investor. Very stern adherents of *laissez-faire* doctrine object not just to the practice of redistributing income, but even to the phrase "distribution of income." They think it implies that income is not purely "earned" but is in part just "received" as a result of social processes rather than pure individual effort. But the social processes are undeniable. So, when John D. Rockefeller told Congress, in all sincerity, that "the good Lord gave me my money," he not only defined regulation as impiety, he denied government's role in the generation of wealth.

Ideological capitalists are like many proponents of abortion in that they are guilty of the neutrality fallacy. Pro-abortion activists worked successfully to impose, by Federal judicial power, the policy of abortion on demand, to impose it in fifty states that did not want such a policy. Those persons should not now argue that their undertaking, unlike that of opponents reacting to them, is "value-free," and does not involve "imposing" values on the community. It is comparably untenable for those who favor a purer capitalism to argue that they, unlike all advocates of different systems, are acting "neutrally" by keeping, or taking, "economics" out of politics, or vice versa.

A famous economist, who has a Nobel Prize and (what is almost as much fun) a regular column in *Newsweek*, recently became so exasperated with me (for some deviation from *laissez-faire* orthodoxy) that he wrote a stiff note. He said that he likes what I write—except when I write about economics. I am too exquisitely polite to have replied that I like what he writes—except when he writes about politics, and he rarely writes about anything else.

When Napoleon tersely summarized his social doctrine in four words—"Careers open to talents"—he was not formulating an employment policy; he was not talking economics. If we are to be properly conscious of our politics, if our politics is to be properly conscious of itself, we must be wide awake to this fact: Choosing an economic system, or choosing substantially to revise significant economic policies, is a political, which means moral, undertaking. It is the authoritative assignment of values, the encouragement of some behavior and values and the discouragement of others.

If conservatism is to engage itself with the way we live now, it must address government's graver purposes with an affirmative doctrine of the welfare state. The idea of such an affirmation may, but should not, seem paradoxical. Two conservatives (Disraeli and Bismarck) pioneered the welfare state, and did so for impeccably conservative reasons: to reconcile the masses to the vicissitudes and hazards of a dynamic and hierarchical industrial economy. They acted on the principle of "economy of exertion," using government power judiciously to prevent less discriminating, more disruptive uses of power. Today, the conservative affirmation of the welfare state should be grounded on, and conservative purposes for the welfare state should be derived from, three additional considerations. They are considerations of prudence, intellectual integrity, and equity. A welfare state is certainly important to, and probably indispensable to, social cohesion, and hence to national strength. A welfare state is implied by conservative rhetoric. A welfare state can be an embodiment of a wholesome ethic of common provision.

The doctrine underlying the political economy of the American welfare state was enunciated in 1877, by Chief Justice Waite, in *Munn* v. *Illinois*. The court upheld an Illinois statute regulating rates in grain elevators, holding that private property

> becomes clothed with a public interest when used in a manner to make it of public consequence, and affect the community at large. When, therefore, one devotes his property to a use in which the public has an interest, he, in effect, grants to the public an interest in that use, and must submit to be controlled by the public for the common good, to the extent of the interest he has thus created.[3]

That opinion proclaimed an idea whose time did not come as social policy for several generations. But it has now come and is not apt to depart. For conservatives to doubt the strength and durability of this consensus is intellectually idle and politically feckless. This consensus cannot, of course, be allowed to erase the distinction between public and private spheres. That distinction is indispensable not only to the preservation of a tolerable degree of liberty, but to the preservation of public-spiritedness as well. It is essential to the habit of subordinating some private interests to the public interest. But conservatives must come to terms with the public's assumption that private economic decisions often are permeated with a public interest and hence are legitimate subjects of political debate and intervention.

Recent years have done damage to the idea that the dangers and discords of life elsewhere cannot get a visa to visit here.

Conservatives know that even in the misnamed "democratic age," democracy has been a rarity, and the "democratic age" is barely two hundred years old—a historical blink. The age was born at approximately the same time as the steam engine, with the age of cheap energy that made rapid economic growth relatively easy. The growth may have made democracy possible because it dampened the most testing social tensions.

The widespread belief that economic growth would democratize prosperity—that a rising tide would raise all boats—reduced the demand for redistributionist politics, in which political decisions would determine the allocation of opportunity and wealth. But when the social question is not just how to bake a larger economic pie, but how to carve the pie, then the stakes of politics become bigger, and politics becomes more bitter. Like it or not, that is a permanent question on the national agenda. It is so because an economic order represents a political choice, and is a government product. We are all in it together, as citizens.

American conservatism needs a Burke, a Disraeli—a self-conscious practitioner who can articulate the principles implicit in the statecraft he practices. Regarding the welfare state, conservatives practice politics more realistically than they preach. In 1953 the conservative party had a President for the first time in a generation, and that party had majorities in both Houses of Congress for the last time in more than a generation. Yet there was no attempt to undo what Franklin Roosevelt had done. Neither, however, was there an attempt to formulate a philosophically conservative rationale and program for the modern state.

A conservative doctrine of the welfare state is required if conservatives are even to be included in the contemporary political conversation. Conservatives need ways to make the welfare state more compatible with conservative governmental values, and to make it more affirmative of conservative social values. Granted, a welfare state can aggravate the centrifugal tendencies of modern society. By enlarging the political allocation of wealth and opportunity, it can raise the stakes, and the temperature, of politics, making the state itself much more a focus of contention than a force of cohesion. But by expressing a limited but clear ethic of common provision, a welfare state can be, on balance, unifying. It can nationalize concern for moderate and cooperative policies to promote the economic growth that alone can pay for general entitlements. A structure of public entitlements can do what private property alone cannot do: it can give everyone a stake in the stability and success of the social system.

What most conservatives know by intuition, and many liberals now know by experience, is this. Government is not efficient at providing goods and services. It is good at writing checks, and at providing incentives and disincentives that cause self-interested persons—that is, almost everybody—to behave in various ways. So a welfare state run on conservative principles will provide the poor with cash to buy necessities from the private sector, thereby reducing the need for an enormous social-service bureaucracy. And a conservative welfare state will provide incentives—such as deductions from taxes for medical-insurance premiums—to cause the private sector to weave much of the net of security that people demand in every developed, industrial society.

In addition to these conservative principles of government, there are social goals for a conservative welfare state. The first is to strengthen what Burke called the "little platoons" that are, even more meaningfully than individuals, the molecular units of society. Conservatives should be leading the fight for a welfare system that supports rather than disintegrates families. The more we learn about the radiating consequences of disintegrated families, the more clearly we can see the social costs—from unemployment to crowded prisons—of neglecting that most

important "little platoon." In addition, a conservative welfare state will use government to combat the tendency of
the modern bureaucratic state to standardize and suffocate
diversity. To give just one example, a conservative welfare state
would give to individuals tax credits—a tax subsidy—to offset
tuition payments to private schools. This incentive to private
education, especially at the secondary level, would stimulate
competition against one of the nation's most powerful lobbies
and its strongest near-monopoly, public education. This is not
to disparage public education. On the contrary, public policy
should encourage a leavening diversity from private sources,
and should encourage bracing competition from private schools,
precisely because education is the most important public business, and because public schools always will and should have
by far the greater number of students.

My purpose here is only to sample the range of possible uses
of assertive government to achieve conservative goals. For
nearly half a century conservatism was, or felt itself to be, in
the political wilderness. Although there were some conservative
Presidents and some conservative legislating majorities in Congress during this period, conservatism generally was a doctrine
in, and of, opposition. During this period it became cranky and
recriminatory. Therefore, a question posed by the coming to
power of self-conscious conservatism is this: Can there be conservatism with a kindly face?

Another question is: can conservatives come to terms with a
social reality more complex than their slogans? Conservatives
rightly stress equality of opportunity rather than equality of
outcomes. Conservatives are, therefore, fond of the metaphor
of a footrace: All citizens should be roughly equal at the start-
ing line of the race of life. But much that we have learned and
continue to learn—and we are learning a lot—about early-
childhood development suggests that "equality of opportunity"

is a much more complicated matter than most conservatives can comfortably acknowledge. Prenatal care (which the "right to life" movement should regard as something of a "right"), infant stimulation, childhood nutrition and especially home environment—all these and other influences affect the competence of a young "runner" as he or she approaches the academic hurdles that so heavily influence social outcomes in America. There is, of course, vast scope for intelligent disagreement as to what can and should be done to make "equality of opportunity" more than an airy abstraction. But surely it is indisputable that "equality of opportunity" can be enhanced by various forms of state action.

The most important reason conservatives should give for their vision of the welfare state is the most important reason for doing anything, politically. It is justice. Saint Thomas Aquinas said that justice, which is giving individuals their due "with constant and perpetual will,"[4] is a "habit" (*habitus*). Justice depends, therefore, on a certain disposition. It depends on—in a sense, it is—a state of mind. A society that is organized socially and justified philosophically the way ours is must take special care to supply itself with the rhetoric, institutions and policies which encourage that state of mind. Neither the spirit of the age nor the premises received from the past (which have produced that spirit) will do the work. The political philosophy of modernity, taking its bearings from the strongest passions, does not emphasize, and so does not nurture, the habit of regarding our fellow citizens as united in a great common enterprise.

Great politics is grounded in a clear vision of the polity. This century's finest political memoirs begin: "All my life I have thought of France in a certain way."[5] The American nation's finest political career derived from Lincoln's refusal to allow his country to be seduced into thinking of itself in an unworthy

way. Americans have had various anxieties about their character's evolving in ways incompatible with the "certain way"
they have thought about America.

In the 1950s, the enormously popular books inciting anxiety
about "conformity"—everyone was reading them—were far
from the first or last symptom of worry about the homogenizing
tendencies of modern life. Uneasiness about America's character, and the liberalism that underlies it, was heard in the Jacksonian argument, and in Henry Adams' assessment of the
"gilded age," and in Woodrow Wilson's lament: "The truth is,
we are all caught in a great economic system which is heart-
less."[6] Such ideas have been less a political persuasion than a
cultural critique, confined to thinkers at the margin of politics.
As Richard Hofstadter wrote:

> In material power and productivity the United States has
> been a flourishing success. Societies that are in such good
> working order have a kind of mute organic consistency.
> They do not foster ideas that are hostile to their funda-
> mental working arrangements. Such ideas may appear, but
> they are slowly and persistently insulated, as an oyster de-
> posits nacre around an irritant.[7]

Still, an irritant to an oyster can become a pearl beyond price,
and there is value to ideas which, although not denouncing the
fundamental working arrangements of a commercial republic,
nevertheless cast a cool eye on the long-term effects of those
arrangements.

Our arrangements may have been ably explicated by those
who arranged them. *Federalist* 51 is, with the possible excep-
tion of *Federalist* 10, the most important short essay on the
American government and psyche. Remember:

> This policy of supplying by opposite and rival interests,
> the defect of better motives . . .[8]

It is almost as though the Founders thought they had devised a system so clever that it would work well even if no one had good motives—even if there was no public-spiritedness. But unfortunately, just as there are social roots of political behavior, there are social consequences of political behavior—and political expectations. A nation that announces, at its outset, that it can dispense with "better motives" than self-interest in politics does not encourage self-restraint, self-denial and moderation in any sphere of life. Drawing upon Montesquieu, many Founders thought that commerce—the submersion of passion and interest in pursuit of private gain—was more reliable than public virtue as a basis of political stability. But real conservatives have said it well and often: Democracy subverts itself if it subverts the habits of self-restraint, self-denial and public-spiritedness. That danger defines the drama of democracy in a commercial nation, a nation devoted to inflaming and satisfying appetites.

Now, just as myth can be conducive to reasonableness in societies, self-interestedness can be conducive to the public interest. The obvious virtue of *laissez-faire* economics is the voluntary performance of many socially useful functions. Its vision of a relatively frictionless mechanism of social adjustment is at once rationalistic and romantic. It is hard to say which is more American, romanticism or capitalism. Perhaps it is wrong, in America, to distinguish them.

Modernity, by assigning to man a clear but demoralizing function as an instrument of production, provoked a romantic reaction, most potently from a romantic masquerading as a "scientific" socialist: Karl Marx. But the case De Tocqueville made for our world should not be dismissed:

> The principle of self-interest rightly understood produces no great acts of self-sacrifice, but it suggests daily small acts of self-denial. By itself it cannot suffice to make a man virtuous; but it disciplines a number of persons in habits of

regularity, temperance, moderation, foresight, self-com-
mand; and if it does not lead men straight to virtue by
the will, it gradually draws them in that direction by
their habits. If the principle of interest rightly understood
were to sway the whole moral world, extraordinary virtues would doubtless be more rare; but I think that gross
depravity would also then be less common. The principle
of interest rightly understood perhaps prevents men from
rising far above the level of mankind, but a great number
of other men, who were falling far below it, are caught
and restrained by it. Observe some few individuals, they
are lowered by it; survey mankind, they are raised.

I am not afraid to say that the principle of self-interest
rightly understood appears to me the best suited of all
philosophic theories to the wants of the men of our time,
and that I regard it as their chief remaining security against
themselves.[9]

I understand, and really am reasonably cheerful about, the
irrevocable triumph of modernity in justifying social orders
based on wide release of passions and appetites. That is why
I am so concerned about the shaping of passions and desires in
the direction of virtue. By virtue I mean nothing arcane or
obscure. I mean good citizenship, whose principal components
are moderation, social sympathy and willingness to sacrifice
private desires for public ends.

There are those who will say, as Hume did, that the principles of civic virtue are noble, "but as these principles are too
disinterested, and too difficult to support, it is requisite to govern men by other passions, and animate them with a spirit of
avarice and industry, art and luxury."[10] And how soothing
modernity is in asserting the easy reconciliation of private pursuits with public exigencies. But some "surgeon general of the
soul," noting the problematic relationship between the premises
of modernity and the social ground of civic virtue, might wish
to place a warning on modern society like that found on cig-

arette packages: Warning—the ethos of this society may be harmful to your moral health.

John Stuart Mill wrote, "The spirit of a commercial people will be, we are persuaded, essentially mean and slavish, wherever public spirit is not cultivated by an extensive participation of the people in the business of government in detail."[11] He may or may not have been correct about his fear and his prescription. But he unquestionably was correct about the need to plan ahead for public-spiritedness.

We need to know more about the policies and processes, the fabric of rights and duties, the sort of involvements in particular institutions, public and private, that are apt to summon the better angels of the citizenry's nature. We need to understand the chemistry of citizenship, the skill of disposing persons to think of public as well as private interests. Unfortunately, the social sciences have lost their nerve—not without reason—at a moment when we need a sociology of civic virtue, of public-spiritedness. Nevertheless, political philosophy must begin with this premise: Reflection about how the individual should live is inseparable from reflection about the nature of the good society. Today we need an argument about the connection between the society we have and the kind of individuals we want American life to nurture. This argument must involve more than the Republican and Democratic arguments about the most expeditious way to orient politics to the increase of material well-being. The argument between Manchester and Massachusetts liberalism is not unimportant in terms of public policy, but it does not reach philosophic fundamentals. All economic arrangements, whatever the mixture of free trade and protection and subsidies and entitlements, should be discussed as expedients. They should be evaluated in terms of the contributions they make to the things we value fundamentally, the things involving important political principles: equality of opportunity, neighborliness, equitable material allocation, happiness, social cohesion, justice. The idea of a finally "correct" equilibrium of ingredients of economic policy—the precisely right recipe of market and state allocations of wealth and opportunity—is a chimera. As Disraeli said, "Finality is not the language of politics."[12]

The question is not does capitalism (or socialism; or a mixed economy) work? Of course it does. So did the Pony Express. The question is what do you mean by "work"? There is more to judging economic arrangements than judging how far, smoothly and fast they expand the Gross National Product. De Tocqueville spoke of "a theory of manufactures more powerful than customs and laws,"[13] and such capitalism has proved to be. It is difficult for statesmen, or anyone else, to measure what De Tocqueville called "the slow and quiet action of society upon itself,"[14] because the action is so slow and quiet. But that action must be watched.

Societies, like individuals, can be, to a considerable extent, defined by their admirations. A society which orients politics to acquisition is apt to be a society in which admiration accrues to the most successful acquirers. Furthermore, a prerequisite of capitalism in the early stages of accumulation is the suppression of spontaneous desire. Democracy and capitalism are compatible only as long as the habits of political and economic self-restraint (deferral of gratification; industriousness; thrift) reinforce one another. The question is what happens when the ethics of a commercial civilization—the relentless manufacturing of appetites, and the incitement to gratify them on credit—undermines self-restraint in political and economic behavior? The essence of childishness is an inability to imagine an incompatibility between one's appetites and the world. Growing up involves, above all, a conscious effort to conform one's appetites to a crowded world. By so thoroughly taking our political, hence our moral, bearings from the low but strong and steady passions, are we in danger of lingering in perpetual childishness? A society that seeks a steady expansion of desires and a simultaneous satisfaction of them may be, at least in the short run, a great place for advertising account executives and manufacturers of small appliances. But over time, it must be unstable domestically and vulnerable internationally.

Concerning vulnerability, consider the following. In the early 1950s, the Western democracies enjoyed overwhelming scientific and technological advantages in nuclear weapons and other weapons and delivery systems. They then decided to rest their security on their technological virtuosity rather than on civic virtue. That is, they decided not to pay the onerous price, in government spending and deprivations of freedom (conscription), that would have been necessary to counter the conventional forces deployed by their adversary, a thoroughly militarized regime dominating the Eurasian landmass. Instead, the Western democracies decided to defend themselves on the cheap, with instruments of mass destruction, so that they could go about the business of liberal democracy: maximizing levels of private consumption and devoting public resources to funding the consumption of the public goods and services dispensed by welfare states.

However, the scientific and technological advantage was short-lived. By the beginning of the 1980s, the Soviet Union enjoyed a clear advantage in theater nuclear forces in Europe and an overwhelming conventional-force advantage. Furthermore, there was rising revulsion in the West against reliance on weapons of mass destruction—a reliance that was, revulsion aside, decreasingly credible. Because of demographic trends, by the end of the 1980s, just in order to maintain current manpower levels, the U.S. armed services will require the voluntary enlistment of a steadily higher percentage of high school graduates not going to college. The services almost certainly will not get that.

To the extent that Western publics achieve what they cur-

rently think they want—a decreased deterrent function for nuclear forces—they must be prepared to do what they have
hitherto been adamantly unwilling to do: increase substantially
their conventional forces. How will liberal democracies square
their need for conventional forces with their aversion to the
coercion of conscription and to an enlarged state share of the
nation's wealth for goods and services—military goods and services—that no one enjoys purchasing? They probably will not
square it. Will liberal democracies, inoculated with years of
rhetoric about the overriding value of individualism and private
gratifications, accept a call from government to the disagreeable collectivism of national service? Probably not.

Having decided at the outset that all men are, self-evidently,
created equal, Americans have spent two centuries pondering
equality. There has never been any doubt that certain inequalities are constitutive of sound social policies; they are prerequisites for desirable social ends. A society determined to have
rapid economic growth through predominantly private market
mechanisms must provide the requisite rewards for the persons
most proficient at generating wealth. That means inequality.
A just society is not one in which the allocation of wealth,
opportunity, authority and status is equal. Rather, it is one in
which inequalities are reasonably related to reasonable social
goals. Therefore justice, as well as elementary utilitarian considerations, requires a hierarchy of achievement. Furthermore,
equality, when defined in terms of rights derivative from passions, is not conducive to community. And questions as to how
much equality of material condition society needs or morality
demands or the economy can stand are less interesting than this
question: How equal a distribution of ideas and sentiments is
needed for social cohesion and all that derives from it? Such
cohesion depends on a revived sense of citizenship. That sense
depends on rehabilitating from the ravages of modern thought
and practice the status of the political vocation and of govern-

ment. The place to begin is with the task of putting economic argument in its place. That place, as Jefferson and Hamilton understood, is within the political argument, and subordinate to political choices. Only then shall we have a politics that nurtures the spiritual in a nation that is predisposed by its modernity toward preoccupation with the material.

CHAPTER SEVEN

Eternity
Warning Time

> *Men are no longer bound together by ideas,*
> *but by interests; and it would seem as if*
> *human opinions were reduced to a sort of*
> *intellectual dust, scattered on every side,*
> *unable to collect, unable to cohere.*
>
> —ALEXIS DE TOCQUEVILLE

AMERICANS, more than most people, believe that history is the result of individual decisions to implement conscious intentions. For Americans, more than most people, history has been that. After all, the nation began, not so long ago, as a virgin continent planted along the Atlantic edge with many people who chose to come there for reasons of religious scruple or other sharply defined convictions.

This sense of openness, of possibility and autonomy, has been a national asset as precious as the topsoil of the Middle West. But like topsoil, it is subject to erosion; it requires tending. And it is not bad for Americans to come to terms with the fact that for them too, history is a story of inertia and the unforeseen. What is most often unforeseen is the inertia.

For the people on the other side of the North Atlantic Basin, the shattering and shaping event of this century was the Great War. It was a vivid demonstration of the melding of inertia and the unforeseen. The boys were to have been "home by Christmas." Instead, the stationary war churned on, the absurdity of the tactics—fighting the machine gun with young men's chests—underscoring the insanely inverse relation between the amount of blood spilled and amount of gains made. When Germany surrendered, there was not a single foreign soldier on German soil.

Americans have suffered no such trauma; no episode has given them such a sense of being playthings of vast, impersonal forces. But increasingly, Americans are anxious. They sense their society becoming a field of impersonal forces, and tending toward entropy. Americans have gone further than a people has ever dared to go in founding a society on thorough-going individualism. Today, the great question is what it was when, in September 1863, Lincoln dedicated a cemetery for young men who had given their last full measure of devotion to something more than individualism. The question is can this nation, or any nation so conceived and so dedicated, long endure? Well, it depends on, among other things, what you mean by this nation, and what you mean by long.

The idea that all political philosophy is a series of footnotes to Plato is especially apt with regard to the recurring theme of decay. "Hard as it may be for a state so framed to be shaken," Plato wrote in *The Republic*, "yet, since all that comes into being must decay, even a fabric like this will not endure forever, but will suffer dissolution."[1] So it has been, and so it is that the mind of the West has been haunted by "the glory that was Greece and the grandeur that was Rome."[2] As this century of unprecedented suffering and danger winds down, few poets are inclined to assure us, as Robert Browning did, "For these things tend still upward, progress is / The law of life, man is not Man as yet."[3]

Every chapter of the history of this century teaches that civilization is more complicated and precarious than hitherto thought. It is maintained by the civilizing discipline of well-practiced politics. And politics needs to be increasingly important as a source of social unity because culture is decreasingly so.

Homer can be said to have been the true founder of his people because he gave them what made them distinctive: their gods, and heroes as incarnations of the virtues. But today there is no canon of books that play the role the Bible and Shakespeare once played in the education of English-speaking people. There are few books which supply civilizing models of virtue and vice, or which make possible a unifying common bond of communication. Somehow, *M*A*S*H* and *Star Wars* cannot. The thinness of the stream of shaping culture is, in part, a function of the fragility of contemporary assumptions and categories. In this age more than in any other it is true that a person cannot imagine what he is going to believe about a lot of things if he just keeps his ears and eyes open. It is peculiar to the modern age that one can say (as Fr. Ronald Knox did), "You do not believe what your grandfathers believed, and have no reason to hope that your grandsons will believe what you do."[4] This is tolerable only up to a point—the point at which political and social consensus becomes dangerously attenuated and citizenship becomes a blurry notion.

A democratic society presupposes only minimal consensus as to the common good; but it presupposes consensus nonetheless. The definition of a polity in terms of comprehensive uniformity of belief has been well and thoroughly discredited, especially by the twentieth century's political invention, totalitarianism. Unity does not require such uniformity; indeed, one powerful lesson of the American experience is that unity is compatible with kinds and degrees of diversity (ethnic, racial, religious) hitherto assumed to be incompatible. The aim of politics is not "the forc't and outward union of cold and neutrall and inwardly divided minds."[5] Rather, it is a warm citizenship, approximating friendship, based on a sense of shared values and a shared fate. It depends, to some extent, on policies which generate the feeling that we are and ought to be in some corporate enterprise that stands for something. The steady amelioration of physical distress by state action has produced societies in which the most important problems are of the spirit. Mankind has needs—call them spiritual, moral, emotional—that may be connected in interesting ways with material conditions but cannot be reduced to physical needs and are ignored by society at its peril.

Among those nonphysical needs is a sense of social warmth, sometimes called "community." When people have an unsatisfied longing for a temperate warmth of community feeling, they become susceptible to the appeal of political leaders who will turn up the temperature—a Hitler assuaging the atomizing effects of military defeat and hyperinflation, a Khomeini bent on retribalizing persons disoriented by the pell-mell modernization of a traditional society.

In its quest for universals—the "rights of man," and all that—eighteenth-century rationalism tried to envision humanity stripped of such supposed inessential attributes as cultural, ethnic and class particularities. The reaction of nineteenth-century romanticism against this was powerful, and the twentieth-century spillover was vicious. Many people found immersion in the broad, bland ocean of "humanity" akin to drowning. The idea of "humanity in general" suggests that the attributes which rationalism rinsed out of political thinking—habits, customs, mores, dispositions—are irrelevancies like chrome on a car, decorative but inessential.

But a person is, in substantial measure, the culture he carries, including the values of the polity in which he is incubated. Hitler's complaint about Jewish "cosmopolitanism" was, in part, a diseased version of the romantic reaction against sterile rationalist politics. A brutal irony is that Jews were hounded both because some were "different" and "unassimilable" and because others were not different enough—they were too representative of Enlightenment values, transcending nationalities. Critics called the subsequent founding of the state of Israel an instance of the "retribalization" of mankind, a retreat from the Enlightenment's noble vision of "humanity in general." A kinder, truer analysis is this: The founding of Israel was an assertion, at once defensive and defiant, of particularity. It represented a coming-to-terms with deep-seated desires and affinities. It was, among other things, an acknowledgment of the political importance of attributes and traditions that rationalism regarded as superficial and inessential.

My political thinking has been defined by simultaneous reflection about the best and the worst in the Western political tradition. But I am bound to say that the worst example—totalitarianism—has been especially influential. Its most lurid eruption was in the middle of Europe, in what was, by many measures, Europe's most educated and generally advanced nation. I have been an almost obsessive student of the Nazi episode, and I believe that when it is properly fathomed, it yields lessons that point toward the political philosophy I have sketched in this volume. However, reflexive reaction to the idea of statecraft-as-soulcraft seems to be "That's what Hitler did!"

My point, remember, is not just that statecraft should be soulcraft. My point is that statecraft *is* soulcraft. It is by its very nature. Statecraft need not be conscious of itself as soulcraft; it need not affect the citizens' inner lives skillfully, or creatively, or decently. But the one thing it cannot be, over time, is irrelevant to those inner lives.

The most dismaying aspect of the quick equation of soulcraft with Hitlerism or totalitarianism generally is that the equation reveals misunderstanding of those phenomena. The argument that any governmental concern with citizens' inner lives carries the germ of Hitlerism suggests that totalitarianism is just statism carried to new extremes. But statism involves respect—perhaps misplaced, or excessive—for the state as an embodiment of national traditions and values. Totalitarianism is decisively different.

Totalitarianism is a siphoning of energy toward the center; it is the absorption of voluntary, intermediary institutions into the state's orbit. But it also is the subordination of the state to a party, the incarnation of the party in a "vanguard" group, and of the group in a leader. It is pure willfulness supplanting the slow socialization of the generations by institutions.

Conservatism, properly understood, begins from premises about man and the natural that are diametrically opposed to the premises of totalitarianisms of the left and the right. To say that statecraft is soulcraft is not to say that the state should be the primary, direct instrument for soulcraft. An aim of prudent statecraft is to limit the state by delegating many of its chores to intermediary institutions. Government can become, to a dangerous degree, an interest group, as self-interested as any other, and more abusive than most. But government can apply to itself a kind of antitrust policy. With all its dimensions, from law through rhetoric, government can encourage strength in private institutions just as surely as totalitarian regimes work to enfeeble such institutions.

Conservative soulcraft has as its aim the perpetuation of free government by nurturing people so they can be comfortable and competent in society. Such soulcraft perpetuates government that is restrained by what dignifies it: legitimizing notions of its origin and mission. Its origin is in the soil of society, from which it grows organically. Its mission is defined by unceasing reflection about a great given: natural right. The soulcraft component of statecraft has one proper aim. It is to maintain the basis of government that is itself governed by the best in a 2,500-year legacy of thought and action—social arrangements known to be right because of what is known about human nature.

When man is defined in terms of his nature, he is prey to

tyrannies that frustrate his nature by making him subservient to the tyrant's will. But worse comes when man is defined not in terms of his nature but in terms of his history. What comes is totalitarianism, which aims to reconstitute man to reduce him to raw material for history's processes and purposes. Thus, for example, Soviet totalitarianism cannot be considered an accident of Marxism, the result of a wrong turn by Lenin or Stalin. It is the result of doing what Marx did when he defined man in terms of man's experience rather than his essence.

The conservatism for which I argue is a "European" conservatism. It is a product of the Europe against which European totalitarians have revolted. It is the conservatism of Augustine and Aquinas, Shakespeare and Burke, Newman and T. S. Eliot and Thomas Mann. It preaches the politics of "degree, priority and place, insisture, course, proportion, season, form, office, and custom . . ."

> O, when degree is shak'd,
> Which is the ladder to all high designs,
> The enterprise is sick . . .
> Take but degree away, untune that string,
> And hark! what discord follows![6]

Hitler, the archetypical totalitarian, understood that total power depends on chaos—not just chaos that facilitates the seizure of power, but permanent chaos that prevents settled laws, habits, mores—any routinization—from impeding the sweep of power. Under totalitarianism, even terror is random.

Hitler, a rootless freebooter (he did not even know who his grandfather was), was a pure radical. August Kubizek, who was a friend of the young Hitler in Linz, recalled (in a chapter titled "Adolph Rebuilds Linz") that for all Hitler's gushing about nature, he felt drawn to hurry home from the landscape to a cityscape: "Here he could give full vent to his mania for changing everything, because a city always had good buildings and bad. He could never walk through the streets without being provoked by everything he saw."[7]

Conservatism inculcates identification with government institutions rooted in national cultures. It envisions a gentle symbiosis between the state and the populace, each shaping and being shaped by the other. Against the disparagement of the state as an instrument of coercion, of class domination or some other partial "interest," conservatism teaches the dignity of government that grows organically from native soil. Hitler, whose unblinking gaze was on "race," had no respect for any state, including Germany's. He spent six formative years in Vienna, capital of an empire cobbled together from 50 million people of disparate political, religious, cultural and linguistic traditions. It was, strictly speaking, Balkanized: Metternich said the Balkans begin in Vienna's Third District. Hitler's Vienna experience underscored his contempt for states, institutions—everything except the primacy of "race." He was, like his wicked predecessor, Napoleon, and like a wicked contemporary, Stalin, an outsider. He replaced state symbols with a party symbol—the swastika—and then replaced the state by the party. His passion for public liturgies, with himself performing sacerdotal functions, found fullest expression at the "First Party Rally of Greater Germany" at Nuremberg in 1938. It featured a sacred relic, the Blood Flag, a party flag that had been dipped in the blood of those killed in the failed *Putsch* in Munich in 1923. At the climactic moment of the rally, a voice proclaimed:

> We salute the dead of the World War. We salute the victims of labor. We salute, above all, the dead of the party struggle.

Notice: The party "above all." The party was hardly a venerable carrier of national traditions. It was just twelve years old when the "thousand-year Reich" began its twelve-year life.

When Hitler joined, he received party card No. 7. The party's treasury contained 7.50 marks. The party was his creation; it was his instrument for capturing and then supplanting the core of the state. He so despised the German state that he served in it only when he was offered an office from which he could subordinate the state to his party. His first state office also was his last: Reichschancellor.

Conservatism envisions the prudent intrusion of mind into the swirl of events. It expresses the modest hope of expanding the efficacy of rationality in a world of flux. Hitlerism, like all totalitarianism, began by postulating the total impotence of mind in the face of vast, impersonal forces. Hitler believed that all major events in history are merely manifestations of the drive for racial self-preservation. In contrast, conservatism teaches respect for the "given" in life, for the inertial forces of history, but by doing so it arms us for creative action in the interstices of large events and strong tendencies. Totalitarianism, married to historicism, stands, as Hitler did, for the forced-draft acceleration of history along a predetermined path.

Conservatism advocates not the subordination of the individual to society, but rather a healthy accommodation between the individual and society's continuousness. So thorough was Hitler's contempt for the value of continuity, he produced a violent rupture of the present from the past, and of the present from the future. He gave no thought to a legitimate transfer of power to another leader; he gave no thought to a political program that would or could continue beyond the hour of his death. Hitlerism was politics as autobiography, the manufacturing of tumultuous politics out of the personal turmoils of an individual. It had the highest possible ratio of personal to institutional influences. It is appropriate that the last substantial opposition to his consolidation of power in 1934 came from conservatives, and that a decade later, conservatives were heavily involved in the attempt to kill him.

The common thread running through the careers of this century's worst history-makers is the conviction that history-making is everything because history makes everything. Nature makes no difference, because man is only what happens to him. Man has no inner gyroscope, no *telos*—nothing that does or should impede or inhibit tyrants. Tyrants thus can treat mankind as so much inert matter into which they, God-like ("And the Lord God formed man of the dust of the ground . . ."), instill life.

Hitler and other villains—Mussolini and Mao, Khomeini and Nasser and Castro and others—have been wind-makers, blowing the masses like dust, giving shape to societies that have become, for one reason or another, invertebrate. A society in which the public turns to the dust of mere "interests" is reduced to hoping that the wind will not rise. Prudence requires measures to encourage citizens to be linked by ideas that give public content to the public mind, and give it in a shape and substance that deflect idle winds.

Biologically, we are directed toward culture; we are pointed beyond our individual existences, toward our species, in the form of our community and progeny. Politically, we should be led up from individualism. De Tocqueville warned that individualism "at first, only saps the virtues of public life; but in the long run it attacks and destroys all others and is at length absorbed in downright selfishness."[8] It is telling that, several generations after De Tocqueville spoke of "mental dust," Emile Durkheim wrote anxiously about modern societies composed of "a dust of individuals." A man without a city, said Aristotle, is either a beast or a god. But of course a *man* without "a city"—a shaping and restraining set of cultural acquisitions—is never a god. What Emerson called "the sovereign individual, free, self-reliant and alone in his greatness" is a dangerous fiction. Individual greatness always is a mystery. However, it never purely is "individual." Greatness never is alone in the

sense of having been produced with no debt to society's nour-
ishing forces. As Learned Hand understood, "You cannot set
up again a Jeffersonian world in separate monads, each looking
up to heaven. For good or evil, man, who must have lived for
a long time in groups, likes too much the warm feeling of his
mental and moral elbows in touch with his neighbors'."[9]

The notion of moral neighborliness is central to an understanding of the idea of a polity, and hence of politics. If you
believe, with Saint Paul, that "our community is already exist-
ing for us in heaven," you may well say to people, as he did,
"Ye are no more strangers and foreigners, but fellow-citizens
with the saints." But before heaven there is the here and now;
and here, now, there are "strangers and foreigners." They do
not have the character of fellow citizens. Robert Peel defined
conservatism as the practice of "that combination of laws, of
institutions, of usages, of habits and of manners which has contributed to mould and form the character of Englishmen."[10]
Conservatives should feel a special responsibility and urgency
about providing and conserving a common character. The
modern state is comprehensively concerned with conditions,
not character. But the processes by which conditions are
changed leave an impress on the character of those involved
in the processes. Certainly the dynamics of capitalist society
undermine the sense of a permanent order in the world, a sense
that is highly useful to the transmission of settled beliefs. And
almost everything of importance that today's hyperactive government does regarding "conditions" divides the polity, because unanimity about particular measures is rare. But an aim
of government—indeed, a prerequisite of popular government—
must be a sense of community rooted in a substantial range of
shared values and aims. Surely it is reasonable to plan and act
on the assumption that a political premise and social ethos
of self-interestedness—"self-interestedness with a good conscience"—requires countervailing influences. Modern demo-

cratic states derive their understanding of themselves from a political philosophy which holds that political powers are limited because political purposes are limited. But a democratic state has power sufficient to the task of promoting a sense of commonality, of common purpose, through a welfare state that embodies an ethic of common provision—an ethic of friendliness, of neighborliness. A democratic state has power sufficient to administer policies regarding abortion, sexual relations and pornography less extreme than today's policies which bespeak the notion that these matters touching the generation of life and the quality of life are matters of indifference to the community. A liberal democratic government has power sufficient systematically to encourage a rational division of social labor between the state and society's "little platoons," and to strengthen those platoons, especially the family.

In the previous two centuries, when most families were where most families had always been—on the land, far from the dissolving forces of urbanity—it was natural to assume that institutions other than those connected with the law would suffice to keep society's integrative impulses sufficiently strong. But in this century of centrifugal urban forces, neglect has told. And expansion of the state in its single-mindedly "materialist," ameliorative mission has aggravated the problem of the state's neglect of soulcraft.

The central government has taken on functions previously performed—if at all—by nonstate institutions, or by local governments, which are those most immediately infused with communitarian values. The institutions that once were most directly responsible for tempering individualism—family, church, voluntary associations, town governments—with collective concerns have come to seem more peripheral. Using government discriminatingly but energetically to strengthen these institutions is part of the natural program of conservatives. Far from being a rationale for statism, the political orientation I praise envisions prophylactic doses of government. It involves the use of government to prevent statism by enhancing the social competence of citizens. In the best and most mature polities, what government does is encourage society to do things through its organic working. Government can do this by enhancing, in many ways, the vigor of those intermediary institutions which shape, support and inspire individuals, drawing persons out of the orbits of individualism and into social relationships. One way that government strengthens such institutions is by not usurping their functions. But that is not the only way. Government can plan positive inducements to vigor.

However, American conservatives are caught in the web of their careless antigovernment rhetoric. They are partially immobilized by their uneasy consciences about government power. This uneasiness derives from their libertarian tendency—from an economic predisposition pressed into service as political philosophy. This question must be asked: If conservatives do not want to use government power in behalf of their values, why do they waste their time running for office? Have they no value other than hostility to government? Or do they value "change," and want to get government out of the way of society's autonomous dynamic of change? Certainly there is a long pedigree to the idea that society's dynamic is necessarily beneficent—"progressive." But it is rash to risk, in advance, a blanket congratulation to society on what this process of change will bring. Certainly conservatives should be specially eager to find occasions for using the power of government to demonstrate that membership in the American polity involves broadly shared values and dispositions. This is an exacting task, but it is the price we pay for not being born mud-turtles or trout or oysters.

Among all the stirring American words, few others are so electrifying as a simple order General George Washington issued on April 30, 1777. The Revolutionary War was about to get serious, and Washington commanded this of his army of fledgling nationalists: "Put none but Americans on guard to-night." It is a fortunate founder who can rely on citizens before he has made a nation. America has always been a fortunate nation, not least because it has been a self-conscious nation. But the dynamic of our society, and its self-conscious commitment to relying on self-interestedness rather than "better motives," has drastically reduced the degree to which Americans are self-conscious about what being an American involves, other than occupancy of a physical locality. Conservatives should be dismayed about that, and should be determined to find political ways to rectify this political defect.

Government is inadequate unless statesmen have a sense of what Shelley called "Eternity warning Time." In the modern age, statesmen should derive a warning from the philosophy of political modernity: If right rests solely on convention, without reference to nature, it rests on opinion which determines convention. Change opinion (broadly construed to include habits, customs, mores) and convention will change, and so will the idea of right. And so will the mind and character of the citizenry. Citizenship is a state of mind, so if the mind is changed enough, the public may still be citizens, but of a different nation. National character is a real thing, molded in part by law and politics, and it is not made of marble.

In an introduction to Walter Bagehot's *The English Constitution*, Lord Balfour, writing with colonial experiences in mind, wrote: "Constitutions are easily copied, temperaments are not; and if it should happen that the borrowed constitution and the national temperament fail to correspond, the misfit may have serious results."[11] But the history of a nation's character and a nation's constitution are distinct; a misfit can develop between a people and a constitution they have inherited, not borrowed. Jefferson wondered: "But is the spirit of the people an infallible, a permanent reliance?" He answered that "the spirit of the times may alter, will alter."[12] Because "national character" is not a concept that lends itself to quantification, it is not the sort of variable with which social scientists enjoy dealing. That is one reason there is reluctance to consider why national character is a variable—why a nation's character varies over time. But the reluctance must be overcome; as Walter Lippmann said, "The acquired culture is not transmitted in our genes, and so the issue is always in doubt."[13]

The late twentieth century needs what the mid–nineteenth century had, a Matthew Arnold to insist that everything connected with culture, from literature through science, depends on a network of received authority. As Learned Hand said, "Life is too short, and experiment too costly, for the individual to verify an appreciable part of what the race has learned. . . . Empiricists in theory we may boast ourselves . . . but practically, we are condemned to be authoritarians, and must guide our lives by the authentic deliverances of accredited sages."[14] Conservatives have a special duty to think about what is accredited, and what should be conserved. It is easy to caricature conservative politics, not only because some conservatives seem to think that thought is somehow anticonservative, but also because there have been so many conservatives for whom thought was an infrequent torture. Lord Liverpool is a fine example of the species. A Frenchman once said that if Lord Liverpool (Prime Minister of Britain 1812–1827) had been present at Creation, he would have exclaimed, "*Mon Dieu, conserve le chaos!*" The development of the ability to distinguish between the good and the traditional was an important accomplishment in the history of the human race. But that invention posed a problem which is inherently perennial: assessing the traditional and deciding which portions of it to relinquish, and which to transmit. There is all the difference in the world between regarding tradition as instrumental in achieving

justice and regarding it as the standard of justice. It is the difference between conservative and reactionary politics.

Conservatism sees tradition as instrumental to, not antitheti-
cal to, reason. Burke was not an irrationalist. His point was not
that reason is impotent or dangerous, or even a weak reed.
Rather, he argued that political reasoning is a social product.
Our forms of political reasoning depend on categories derived
from the Greeks, Romans and Jews who were present at the
creation of the tradition we call Western civilization. Our political reasoning has been shaped by institutions, religions, lit-
eratures and other contingencies of national cultures. Our political reasoning is expressed in categories that are and ought to
be somewhat parochial—native flowers sprung from native soils.

Burke did not so much define the sphere of reasoning less
spaciously than modern liberals do; rather, he defined reasoning
differently. He understood that cognitive processes, of persons
or groups, are not autonomous. Modern philosophy has not
often been hospitable to "the thought that processes of governance could be both rational and deeply rooted in social
practice."[15] But "rational governance is not some strange exotic
plant that we need to visit some intellectual conservatories to
see."[16] And "It is a strange prejudice that precludes the classification as rational of any processes of development, in science,
morals or whatever, that cannot be managed in one single generation and therefore require trans-generational mutational
processes of intellectual reproduction. It is a strange prejudice
that restricts the designation of rational results to those that
could be encompassed, beginning with accepted procedures, by
one person in one life-time."[17]

The philosophy as well as the history of the physical sciences suggests that even in such realms of individual genius,
knowledge is "essentially a communal institution."[18] Hegel has
won and Kant has lost, in this sense: We no longer believe that

our wellsprings of thought and volition are independent of our histories, and the histories of our societies.

Today, when the social sciences do their work well, they convey a sense of complexity and necessity in the life of society. In this regard, not even journalism is invariably a net loss to understanding. It too occasionally helps people understand that the milieu in which politicians operate is not the light, open space of Newtonian philosophy; rather, the milieu is more the thick, clinging mud in which Darwin embedded mankind's sense of itself. Liberalism thinks of society too much the way the eighteenth century thought of the heavens (and society): as clear, tidy and timeless. Liberalism is political astronomy—anachronistic astronomy, unaware that even the planets do more wobbling and wandering and banging about than the eighteenth century thought. Conservatism is political biology. It emphasizes the indeterminateness, the complexity of things, and the fact that there is more to a social system than meets the eye.

Conservatism also teaches that there is more to a social system than can be presumed. Madison acknowledged, rather coolly, that some human qualities justify "a certain portion of esteem and confidence" and that "Republican government presupposes the existence of these qualities in a higher degree than any other form."[19] Presupposes? Those qualities must be willed. It is folly to will an end but neglect to will the means to the end. The presuppositions of our polity must be supplied, politically.

I call what I advocate "conservative" soulcraft only because its aim is conservation. It pertains to the conservation of values and arrangements that are not subjects of day-to-day debate. Is Mr. Will advocating government that promotes things Mr. Will favors? Yes—up to a point. But the point is well short of favoring government that intervenes to stack the deck in everyday arguments about the shifting practical programs of the political parties. It would be peculiar to accuse—I guess that is the proper word—Aristotle of having favored a state that reflects an Aristotelean view of reality, and is congenial to Aristotelean values. So accused, Aristotle would have said, cheerfully: "Yep, you bet—guilty!" We lesser mortals, who plug along at the enterprise begun in Greece, trying to grapple with the great questions of political philosophy, do so for the same reason the giants of the tradition have done so: we want to improve the likelihood of government that is, by our lights, reasonable.

Political philosophy is a political act. But there are many levels to the game of politics. Soulcraft should concern politics at a high level of generality. It should be concerned not with particular programs but with criteria for judging programs.

The aim of education is to teach people how to think, not what to think. We should not tolerate teachers who use their positions to propagandize. But neither should we tolerate teachers who are indifferent to the kinds of judgments students come to, or the students' ways of coming to them.

And, if people think clearly, there are many conclusions to which they will not come. The aim of statecraft as soulcraft is not to promote a particular view of Social Security, or the Federal Reserve Board, or public works, or nuclear deterrence, or similar practicalities of an ongoing polity. The question of the extent to which government should, say, be involved in allocating medical care, or the more general question of the optimum equilibrium of liberty and equality in society's evolving program of distributive justice—such questions should be the subject of unending debate, and will inevitably be the issues around which our partisanships are organized. Various parts of government under the control of this or that party will lean this way or that in these arguments. But the state in its ongoing capacity is not a partisan in such arguments. It is, however, a permanent, unobtrusive partisan on behalf of the personal traits, social mores and institutional processes that healthy partisanship presupposes. It must be so because freedom is a discipline.

To begin at the beginning of politics is to talk about talk, about the prevailing political idiom, the traditional idiom of democracy. T. S. Eliot's famous axiom—that mankind cannot stand too much reality—is an important political truth. Democratic publics in modern states flinch from facing truths about their condition, and perhaps they should be spared some truths. But politics is 95 percent talk, and if we talk too unrealistically, we will get government that is unnecessarily unrealistic. It is realistic to say that government generally is a dance, a minuet, of small minorities. The judgment of small minorities, in government and out, is almost always decisive. Because of the scale of modern government, the great majority of the people know relatively little about what the government is doing, at least until it has done it, and generally do not know much about it even then. Indeed, it is at least arguable that a century ago, before the expansion of print journalism and before the invention of broadcast journalism, the great majority of the people knew about a larger fraction of what their government was doing than the great majority knows today.

Government is becoming complex much faster than public opinion can become complex. Indeed, as long as people have more to do than think about government, there will be no "public opinion" about most matters of decision in a large state. There is today no "public opinion," in a meaningful sense, about range limits on cruise missiles, or dairy subsidies, or steel import quotas, or cargo-preference legislation. There are, of course, lots of little "publics," organized, attentive and clamorous. The fundamental goal of modern liberalism has been equality, and it has given us government that believes in the moral equality of appetites. The result is a government that is big but not strong; fat but flabby; capable of giving but not leading. It is invertebrate government, a servile state that is part cause and part consequence of the degradation of the democratic dogma. That degradation is apparent in the fact that today, there is no higher praise for a government or governor than to say that it or he or she is "responsive"—that is, quick to respond to received demands. But a government obsessed with responsiveness is incapable of leadership. Leadership is, among other things, the ability to inflict pain and get away with it—short-term pain for long-term gain. Liberalism, which is the politics of the pleasure principle, has made government the servant of consumption and, not coincidentally, the enemy of investment, which is the deferral of gratification. The one thing we do not have is strong government.

To revitalize politics and strengthen government, we need to talk about talk. We need a new, respectful rhetoric—respectful, that is, of the better angels of mankind's nature. It must be more Ciceronian, more Lincolnesque, less Madisonian and Marshallean. Talk matters, because mankind is not just matter, not just a machine with an appetitive ghost in it. We are not what we eat. We are, to some extent, what we and our leaders—the emblematic figures of our polity—say we are.

A society that says in its founding philosophy, clearly and often, that public-spiritedness is unnatural should be especially eager to nurture it, hard and often. Perhaps it would be good if modern men were "the hollow men, the empty men." Hollow spaces can be creatively filled. Unfortunately, modern man has undergone a mischievous taxidermy; he is stuffed to the bursting point with a dangerous idea. It is the idea that self-interestedness is sufficient to keep society's clockwork mechanism ticking over, and that whatever is wrought by this dynamic should be welcomed by "progressive" people.

We hope to be governed by the wisest; we insist that whoever governs does so by consent; presumably we want elites of character as well as achievement. But the premises of our political order do not serve that political objective. We debase government by defining it in cold, forbidding categories, as "the monopolizer of legitimate coercion," or "the supreme arbiter of power." We enhance government's prestige by connecting the idea of legitimate government with the idea of appropriate ends for political activity. The idea of legitimacy should not be connected merely with the notion of the origin of legitimate power in the consent of the governed. The basic political right is to good government, not self-government. Of course we believe, with passion and reason, that self-government is instrumental to good government, and that individual wills should be expressed regularly and with effect. However, we should not believe that political philosophy begins and ends with arguments about origins and procedures. That belief is a by-product of the assumption that polities are produced the way corporations are, by contracts, and that citizens are whirling atoms that choose to associate in minimal regulation for self-interested reasons. But human nature and civil society are too intricate to be explained or guided by a philosophy that says all solid interests are private interests and all reasoning is individual, not social. Such a philosophy leads to the expression of all social issues in the language of individual rights. That, in turn, gives rise to the belief that all social arguments can be cast as conflicts of individual rights, and that all such conflicts can and should be adjudicated. This raises the general level of truculence in civic relations, and tends to reduce the state to paralysis.

To escape from that intellectual and political *cul de sac* it is necessary to begin correctly, with the notion that government, although of human manufacture, is "natural." It is as natural to man as clothes and shelter because it serves needs that are natural to man. A well-governed polity clothes and shelters the individual, enveloping him in a rich weave of relationships—rights, restraints, duties, privileges, customs, mores—that shape his disposition, buttressing what is best in him and tempering what is worst. This should work to discourage certain lurid diversities—some base or vicious tendencies. However, it also should leave wide scope for diversity. In fact, it should promote a rich diversity because it bears always in mind the enhancement of excellence, and individuals have different faculties that point toward different forms of fulfillment natural to them.

The variety of human capacities at any moment in any society is historically conditioned; therefore the range of suitable forms of political association also is conditioned. Political philosophy for all seasons must consist of quite important but quite general propositions. The public philosophy appropriate for a particular polity can be more specific, but there are quickly reached limits to how far one can usefully venture away from broad propositions when discussing the most eligible forms of political association for polities generally. Try to formulate political prescriptions that would have been true and useful for Henry II's England, Cromwell's England, Wellington's England and Attlee's Britain; or for Louis XIV's France and for De Gaulle's France; or for Cotton Mather's America, Andrew Jackson's America and Lyndon Johnson's America. What is always true is this: In the struggle for human improvement, ground is not only hard to gain but also hard to hold.

"Civilization," wrote William James, "is always in need of being saved. The nation blest above all nations is she in whom the civic genius of the people does the saving day by day, by acts without external picturesqueness; by speaking, writing, voting reasonably; by smiting corruption swiftly; by good temper between parties; by the people knowing true men when they see them, and preferring them as leaders to rabid partisans or empty quacks."[20] When people habitually behave well, we say that their virtue is "second nature to them." To understand such habits, we require more sociological and less institutional discussion of politics. We need no less attention to the separation of powers, First Amendment law and other facets of the government's role as mediator of conflict; but we do need more attention to the social roots of behavior, more thought about the habits and dispositions that shape society and its conflicts. The spur to such discussion should be a sharp sense of something this country, and this century, teaches: the perishableness of things. All things can pass away, including a citizenry's sense of what kind of people they want to be. So a nation requires constant philosophic contemplation about its ends. But in this country, with the high drama of its founding moment and the articulateness of its Founders, contemplation of ends involves—in fact, must begin with—contemplation of beginnings.

America's Centennial and Bicentennial celebrations differed in one striking particular. In 1876, the Centennial was resolutely forward-looking. It focused on the latest machinery. But in 1976, the public's imagination was caught only by an elegant anachronism, the "tall ships." It is possible to put a positive cast on this contrast. In the last century Americans have learned to look back. Looking forward is natural and easy; the future is coming, whether we like it or not, and it will be a realm of action. Looking back is optional; it is an acquired taste and a learned skill. But is the requisite reflectiveness in evidence? Nostalgia is sterile when it reflects only a failure of nerve, a flinching from an arduous present or a daunting future. We need an intellectual, not a sentimental encounter with our past—with the mental world that produced the present world.

It has been said that the trouble with the younger generation is that it has not read the minutes of the last meeting. But no generation is "the younger generation" for long. Soon it is among the older generations, and it is too busy—or too weary, or too complacent—to worry about all that has gone before. In all societies, but especially in an up-and-doing-with-a-heart-for-any-fate society such as ours is—or at any rate, as ours has been—there is a preoccupation with the new. As a result, there

is little attention to renewal. But the second law of thermo-
dynamics has a political analogue: social systems too tend to
run down to entropy. The fuel that carries a social system forward is tradition.

Tradition is not just what is preserved by transmission. It
also is the mode of transmission. It is, therefore, a skill, a form
of mastery. Modern intellectuals believe it their vocation to be
"critical" in a narrow sense. They have adopted an adversary
stance toward all that is received, because things received are
not pure products of will, and thus limit freedom's sphere.
Hence, much more intellectual zest has been invested in intellectual destruction than in conservation. The most important
human task—the one to which most people and institutions de-
vote most energy—is transmission. However, in the last two
centuries—since intellectuals became a self-conscious class with
a sense of vocation—Western society has been intellectually
negligent. It has stopped taking seriously, and hence has, ef-
fectively, stopped transmitting, the theories of the political
philosophers who came before modernity. Society has thereby
deprived itself of a vantage point from which to judge its pre-
dominant thought and edit its practices. By its intellectual com-
placency, society has impoverished its sense of political possibilities. A polity and the persons in it are defined and shaped
together and simultaneously. By thinning its intellectual life,
society has enfeebled its ability to formulate purposes that enable persons to live the most eligible lives, harmoniously.

Today's challenge is to enlarge, by lengthening, the cultural
memory of our society. The aim should be to nurture a sense
of continuity with the rich tradition of political philosophy,
from Aristotle to Burke. Relatively recently—at the time of
Machiavelli and Hobbes—we took a sharp fork in the intellectual road. It is time to retrace our cultural steps, and rethink
what we think.

A theme of modern American historiography is that something epochal occurred about 1890, when the frontier was "closed." Certainly something changed—some source of energy, some agreeable itch or tingle in the nation's soul—when the age of physical exploration ended. But, to recur to the proposition with which I began, a nation is not a physical thing. A nation offers limitless scope for moral explorations.

> We shall not cease from exploration
> And the end of all our exploring
> Will be to arrive where we started
> And know the place for the first time.[21]

In politics "the place" is a mental habitat, an intellectual and moral landscape. To know clearly, perhaps even for the first time, the defective philosophic premises of our nation should not mean loving the nation less. However, to know the thought that launched the nation is to know actions necessary to sustain the nation. Some actions, reflecting mature second thoughts, must compensate for the defects of the first thought. Because a nation is, to some extent, a state of mind, knowing a nation in a new way makes the nation into a new place. What is called for is a contemplative, a philosophic turn of mind.

The Western political tradition did not begin in Philadelphia or Florence. It began in Athens, and has been repeatedly enriched, as by Burke. An open-minded encounter with that tradition in all its richness will show the necessity of statecraft that is conscious of itself as, and has a good conscience about, soulcraft. "A soul is but the last bubble of a long fermentation in the world," Santayana wrote, adding: "This consciousness that the human spirit is derived and responsible, that all its functions are heritages and trusts, involves a sentiment of gratitude and duty which we may call piety."[22] That consciousness should be the animating force for statecraft that is soulcraft.

In a world that is increasingly inhospitable to the ideas and disciplines of liberty, this Republic continues to live improvidently off a dwindling legacy of cultural capital which was accumulated in sterner, more thoughtful eras. That legacy is a renewable resource, but it will not regenerate spontaneously. Regeneration is a political choice, a political chore. If this Republic is to long endure, it must work to improve the actuarial odds against the survival of civility in an untamed world. The way to begin is by understanding this: By not drawing deeply enough from the Western political tradition, this nation has acquired political values and practices which involve a disproportionate individualism and an inadequate sense of human beings as social creatures. The older, richer part of the Western political tradition is now too remote for our own good. But a tradition need not remain as remote as time and negligence have made it. If the wine of the Western tradition has become watery, let us pour some of the vintage that is in the old bottles. It is strong stuff and gives a bracing sense of the dignity of the political vocation, that vocation which is more than a mere partnership in low concerns and vagrant desires. It is, rather, a partnership in making the most of our finest potentialities, and doing so the only way we can: cooperatively. It is the collaborative adventure of trying to measure up to the better angels of our nature.

Politics involves an endless agenda of arduous choices; it can be thrilling and noble. Certainly a sense of the complexity and majesty of politics is indispensable to the care of our time.

Acknowledgments

The genesis of this book was the Godkin Lectures I delivered at Harvard University in October 1981. I am sensible of the compliment conferred by the invitation to deliver the Lectures. To the honor inherent in receiving the hospitality of Harvard is added the distinction of following in the footsteps of the distinguished lecturers who have preceded me to the Godkin lectern. I want to thank Dean Graham Allison, the John F. Kennedy School of Government and all others responsible for the invitation. The finest gift that can come to a writer is an occasion for committing to paper thoughts that might otherwise have remained unthought, or unwritten. For some of us, the process of thinking is inseparable from the process of writing.

Erwin Glikes, my editor, Dusa Gyllensvard, my assistant, and James A. Miller, my friend, made these processes more fruitful.

The contents of this volume constitute a complaint against the modern world. And in this, the "first modern nation," a nation notable for its reverence for its Founding Fathers, my

167

argument comes close to filial impiety. If *lèse majesté* is possible in a republic, I may be committing it. But in another sense, this book is an act of filial piety. My father is a philosopher. These thoughts are my small homage to his noble profession and example. His is a life of quiet insistence on the importance of asking the important questions. I only regret that he asks and answers them so much better than I.

Notes

Epigraph: Marcus Tullius Cicero, *The Republic,* I, xxv 39, The Loeb Classical Library edition, C. W. Keyes, trans. (Cambridge, Mass.: Harvard University Press, 1928), p. 65

CHAPTER ONE: THE CARE OF OUR TIME

Epigraph: Edmund Burke, address "Doctrines of the Old Whigs," *An Appeal from the New to the Old Whigs,* in *The Works of the Right Honorable Edmund Burke* (London: F., C. & J. Rivington, Ltd., 1808), vol. 6, p. 207

1. Walter Berns, *Freedom, Virtue and the First Amendment* (Chicago: Henry Regnery Co., 1965), p. 247
2. Daniel Patrick Moynihan, from a review of John Kenneth Galbraith, *A Life in Our Times* (New York: Houghton Mifflin Co., 1981), *The New Yorker,* August 10, 1981, p. 103
3. Abraham Lincoln, Address Before the Wisconsin State Agricultural Society, Milwaukee, Wisconsin, September 30, 1859, in *The Collected Works of Abraham Lincoln,* Roy P. Basler, ed. (New Brunswick, N.J.: Rutgers University Press, 1953), vol. III, pp. 481–82
4. Lincoln, *ibid.*
5. Burke, *ibid.,* p. 97
6. Burke, *Reflections on the Revolution in France, ibid.,* vol. 5, p. 156

7. Justice Felix Frankfurter, *West Virginia State Board of Education* v. *Barnette*, 319 U.S. 624 (1943) 655

CHAPTER TWO: THE DEFECT

Epigraph: James Madison, *The Federalist*, Jacob E. Cooke, ed. (Middletown, Conn.: Wesleyan University Press, 1961), No. 51, p. 349
1. Marcus Tullius Cicero, *De Officiis*, John Higginbotham, ed. (London: Faber & Faber, Ltd., 1967), Book III, ch. 5, sec. 24, p. 144
2. John Marshall, in the Virginia Ratifying Convention, 1788
3. Burke, "Burke's Personal Defense," *An Appeal from the New to the Old Whigs*, in *The Works of the Right Honorable Edmund Burke* (London: F., C. & J. Rivington, Ltd., 1808), vol. 6, p. 80
4. Burke, "Doctrines of the Old Whigs," *ibid.*, p. 218
5. Burke, *Reflections on the Revolution in France, ibid.*, vol. 5, pp. 183–84
6. Burke, "Doctrines of the Old Whigs," *An Appeal from the New to the Old Whigs, ibid.*, vol. 6, p. 218
7. Immanuel Kant, *Fundamental Principles of the Metaphysics of Ethics*, Otto Manthy-Zorn, trans. (New York: D. Appleton-Century Co., 1938), p. 65
8. Thomas Hobbes, *Leviathan* (Oxford: Basil Blackwell, Ltd., 1960), ch. 8, p. 46
9. David Hume, *A Treatise of Human Nature*, L. H. Selby-Bigg, ed. (Oxford: Clarendon, 1896), II, iii, 3
10. Jeremy Bentham, *An Introduction to the Principles of Morals and Legislation*, Wilfrid Harrison, ed. (New York: Macmillan, 1948), ch. 1, p. 1
11. Alexis de Tocqueville, *Democracy in America*, The Henry Reeve Text, Francis Bowen, ed. (New York: Alfred A. Knopf, Vintage Books, 1958), vol. I, p. 255
12. Sir William Blackstone, *Commentaries on the Laws of England*, William G. Hammond, ed. (San Francisco: Bancroft Whitney, 1890), vol. I, 47
13. John Marshall as quoted by Robert Faulkner, *The Jurisprudence of John Marshall* (Princeton, N.J.: Princeton University Press, 1968), ch. II, p. 45
14. Justice Oliver Wendell Holmes, *Abrams* v. *United States*, 250 U.S., 616, 630, 631 (1919)
15. David Hume, cited in Robert S. Hill, "David Hume," *History of Political Philosophy*, Leo Strauss and Joseph Cropsey, eds. (Chicago: Rand McNally & Co., 1963), p. 508
16. Benedict Spinoza, *Ethics*, I, iii, Preface, in *The Chief Works of*

Benedict Spinoza, R. H. M. Elwes, trans. and intro. (New York: Dover, 1951)

17. Adam Smith, *The Theory of Moral Sentiments* (Indianapolis: Library Classics, 1969), p. 25

18. Thomas Paine, *The Complete Writings of Thomas Paine,* Philip S. Foner, ed. (New York: Citadel Press, 1945), vol. I, p. 359

19. Jeremy Bentham, *Principles of Legislation,* C. M. Atkinson, ed., 2 vols. (London: Oxford University Press, 1914), vol. I, p. 164

20. John Adams, Letter to Abigail Adams, May 12, 1780, in *Adams Family Correspondence,* L. H. Butterfield and Marc Friedlaender, eds. (Cambridge, Mass.: Harvard University Press, 1973), vol. III, pp. 341–42

21. Thomas Hobbes, cited, Sheldon S. Wolin, *Politics and Vision* (Boston: Little, Brown and Co., 1960), p. 253

22. Madison, *ibid.,* No. 10, p. 65

23. Madison, *ibid.,* No. 51, p. 349

24. Madison, *ibid.,* No. 10, pp. 63–64

25. John Locke, "Of the Ends of Political Society and Government," *Locke's Two Treatises of Government,* Peter Laslett, ed. (Cambridge, Great Britain: The University Press, 1960), ch. IX, p. 368

26. Madison, *ibid.,* p. 59

27. Madison, *ibid.,* p. 58

28. Madison, *ibid.,* p. 61

29. Madison, *ibid.*

30. Edmund Burke, "Thoughts on French Affairs" (1791), *ibid.,* vol. VII, p. 42

31. Alexis de Tocqueville, *ibid.,* vol. II, pp. 122–23

CHAPTER THREE: OUT OF THE WILDERNESS

Epigraph: Ralph Waldo Emerson, *The Journals of Ralph Waldo Emerson,* Robert N. Linscott, ed. (New York: Random House, The Modern Library, 1960), p. 394

1. Stephen A. Douglas, from an 1860 speech published in a pamphlet by the Illinois Republican State Central Committee titled "The Political Record of Stephen A. Douglas," in Harry Jaffa, *Crisis of the House Divided* (Seattle: University of Washington Press, 1973), p. 115

2. Abraham Lincoln, from a speech at Peoria, Illinois, October 16, 1854, in *The Collected Works of Abraham Lincoln,* Roy P. Basler, ed. (New Brunswick, N.J.: Rutgers University Press, 1953), vol. II, p. 255

3. Douglas, as quoted from The Seventh Debate, October 15, 1858, *ibid.,* vol. III, p. 286

4. Lincoln, First Debate with Stephen A. Douglas at Ottawa, Illinois, August 21, 1858, *ibid.*, p. 27

5. Lincoln, from The Second Annual Message to Congress, December 1, 1862, *ibid.*, vol. V, p. 527

6. James Monroe, in *The Writings of James Monroe*, Stanislaus M. Hamilton, ed. (New York: G. P. Putnam's Sons, 1902), vol. 6, p. 340

7. Thomas Jefferson, Letter to Thomas Law, June 13, 1814, in *The Life and Selected Writings of Thomas Jefferson*, Adrienne Koch and William Peden, eds. (New York: Random House, The Modern Liibrary, 1944), pp. 636–39

8. Jefferson, *ibid.*

9. Jefferson, *ibid.*

10. Jefferson, *ibid.*

11. Jefferson, *ibid.*

12. Robert Penn Warren, *The Legacy of the Ciivil War: Meditations on the Centennial* (New York: Random House, Vintage Books, 1964), p. 84

13. Gertrude Stein, cited in Robert Hughes, *The Shock of the New* (New York: Alfred A. Knopf, 1981), p. 56

14. John Osborne, *Luther* (London: Faber & Faber, 1961), p. 102

15. Peter Gay, "Introduction: Freud/For the Marble Tablet," in *Berggasse 19: Sigmund Freud's Home and Offices, Vienna 1938, The Photographs of Edmund Engelman* (New York: Basic Books, 1976), p. 35

16. Louis MacNeice, *Poems, 1925–1940* (New York: Random House, 1960), p. 78

17. Walter Pater, *The Renaissance: Studies in Art and Poetry*, from the Conclusion of the 1893 text, Donald L. Hill, ed. (University of California Press, 1981)

18. D. H. Lawrence, *The White Peacock*, Harry T. Moore, gen. ed., Matthew J. Bruccoli, textual ed. (Carbondale and Edwardsville: Southern Illinois University Press, 1966), pt. ii, ch. 2, p. 161

19. Lionel Trilling, *Beyond Culture: Essays on Literature and Learning* (New York: The Viking Press, 1965), p. xvii

20. Trilling, *ibid.*, p. 3

21. Paul Cézanne, cited in Hughes, *ibid.*, p. 125

22. Cézanne, cited, *ibid.*, p. 124

23. Mark Rothko, cited, *ibid.*, p. 262

24. Percy Bysshe Shelley, *Prometheus Unbound*, III, iii, 193, in *Shelley's Poetry and Prose*, selected and edited by Donald H. Reiman and Sharon G. Powers (New York: W. W. Norton & Co., Inc., 1977), p. 194

25. D. H. Lawrence, *Women in Love* (Franklin Center, Pennsylvania: Franklin Library, 1979 ed.), ch. 13, p. 144

26. Alexis de Tocqueville, *Democracy in America*, The Henry Reeve Text, rev. by Francis Bowen; Phillips Bradley, ed. (New York: Alfred A. Knopf, 1963), vol. II, p. 334

27. Emerson, *ibid.*, p. 152

CHAPTER FOUR: SECOND NATURE

Epigraph: Samuel Taylor Coleridge, "Zapolya" Prelude, *The Poetical Works of Samuel Taylor Coleridge*, James Dykes Campbell, ed. (London: Macmillan & Co., Ltd., 1906), p. 406

1. Edmund Burke, *Reflections on the Revolution in France*, in *The Works of the Right Honorable Edmund Burke* (London: F., C. & J. Rivington, Ltd., 1808), vol. 5, pp. 122–23

2. Burke, cited, "Observations on a Late Publication intitled 'Present State of the Nation' " (1769), *ibid.*, vol. 2, p. 170

3. George Santayana, *The Works of George Santayana* (New York: Charles Scribner's Sons, 1933), vol. IV, *The Life of Reason*, p. 139

4. Thomas Jefferson, *Notes on Virginia*, in *The Life and Selected Writings of Thomas Jefferson*, Adrienne Koch and William Peden, eds. (New York: Random House, The Modern Library, 1944), p. 275

5. Jefferson, cited in *American Political Thought*, Morton J. Frisch and Richard G. Stevens, eds. (New York: Charles Scribner's Sons, 1971), p. 37

6. *Plyler v. Doe*, 102, S. CP. 2382, 2397 (1982)

7. *Ibid.*, at 2397

8. *Brown v. Board of Education*, 347 U.S. 483, 493 (1954)

9. *Abingdon School District v. Schemp*, 374 U.S. 203, 230 (1963) (Brennan, J., concurring)

10. *Ambach v. Norwick*, 441 U.S. 68, 76 (1979)

11. *Ibid.*, at 77

12. John Adams, cited, Clinton Rossiter, *Conservatism in America*, 2nd ed., rev. (New York: Random House, Vintage Books, 1962), p. 111

13. First U.S. Congress, Third Article of the Northwest Ordinance, Continental Congress, 1787

14. Daniel J. Boorstin, *The Americans: The Colonial Experience* (New York: Random House, 1958), pp. 179–80

15. Boorstin, *The Americans: The National Experience* (New York: Random House, 1965), pp. 153, 155

16. California State Constitution, Article IX, Section I

17. Jefferson, Letter to Edward Carrington, January 16, 1787, in *The Life and Selected Writings of Thomas Jefferson, ibid.*, p. 411

18. Jefferson, First Inaugural Address, 1801, in *The Complete Thomas Jefferson*, Saul K. Padover, ed. (New York: Tudor Publishing Co., 1943), p. 386

19. Jefferson, Letter to William C. Jarvis, Monticello, September 28, 1820, n *The Writings of Thomas Jefferson*, Ford Leicester, ed. (New York: G. P. Putnam's Sons, 1892–99), vol. 10, p. 161

20. Jefferson, Letter to George Washington from Paris, January 4, 1786, in *Writings of Thomas Jefferson*, Andrew A. Lipscomb, ed. (Washington, D.C.: Thomas Jefferson Memorial Society, 1904), pp. 24–25

21. John Marshall, Letter to Charles Mercer, April 7, 1827, in *The Jurisprudence of John Marshall*, Robert K. Faulkner (New Brunswick, N.J.: Princeton University Press, 1968), p. 143

22. Marshall, *ibid*.

23. David Hume, *Philosophical Essays on Morals, Literature, and Politics*, First American Edition (Georgetown, D.C.: W. Duffy, 1817), vol. I, essay XII, p. 471

24. Hume, cited in Robert S. Hill, "David Hume," *History of Political Philosophy*, Leo Strauss and Joseph Cropsey, eds. (Chicago: Rand McNally, 1963), p. 511

25. Justice Oliver Wendell Holmes, in *Lochner* v. *New York*, 198 U.S. 45 (1905), p. 76

26. Burke, *Correspondence*, Charles William, Earl Fitzwilliam and Lt. Gen. Sir Richard Bourke, K.C.B., eds. (London: 1844), vol. I, p. 332

27. Lon Fuller, *The Morality of Law* (New Haven: Yale University Press, 1964), p. 5

28. Fuller, *ibid*., pp. 5–6

29. Fuller, *ibid*., p. 9

30. Fuller, *ibid*.

31. Fuller, *ibid*.

32. Fuller, *ibid*., pp. 9–10

33. Fuller, *ibid*., p. 10

34. Fuller, *ibid*., p. 17

35. John Stuart Mill, *Utilitarianism, Liberty and Republican Government*, A. D. Lindsay, ed. (London: J. M. Dent and Sons, Ltd., 1962), p. 73

36. James Fitzjames Stephen, *A History of Criminal Law in England* (London, 1883), quoted in Leon Radzinowicz, *Sir James Fitzjames Stephen and His Contribution to the Development of Criminal Law* (Seldon Society Lecture) (London: Bernard Quaritch, 1957), pp. 229–30

37. Jefferson, in *The Life and Selected Writings of Thomas Jefferson, ibid*., p. 274

38. Justice Felix Frankfurter, *W. Va. State Board of Education* v. *Barnette*, 319 U.S. 624 (1943) 655

39. Alexis de Tocqueville, *Democracy in America*, The Henry Reeve Text, rev. by Francis Bowen, Phillips Bradley, ed. (New York: Alfred A. Knopf, 1963), vol. I, p. 46

40. Justice John Harlan, *Cohn* v. *California*, 403 U.S., 24, 1971

41. Aristotle, *Politics*, The Loeb Classical Library Edition, 1253a, 30–33, H. Racklan, trans. (Cambridge, Mass.: Harvard University Press, 1950), bk. I, ch. 2, p. 13

42. Santayana, *ibid.*, p. 132

43. Learned Hand, *The Spirit of Liberty*, Irving Dilliard, ed. (New York: Alfred A. Knopf, 1952), p. 32.

44. Burke, *Reflections on the Revolution in France*, *ibid.*, vol. 5, p. 151

45. Burke, *ibid.*, p. 152

46. Hand, *ibid.*, p. 113

47. Burke, *ibid.*, p. 126

CHAPTER FIVE: THE BROKEN CHAIN

Epigraph: Edmund Burke, *Reflections on the Revolution in France* (1790), in *The Works of the Right Honorable Edmund Burke* (London: F., C. & J. Rivington, Ltd., 1808), vol. 5, p. 37

1. Daniel J. Boorstin, *The Americans: The Colonial Experience* (New York: Random House, 1958), p. 555

2. Boorstin, *ibid.*, p. 1

3. Henry Adams, *The Education of Henry Adams* (Cambridge, Mass.: The Riverside Press, 1961), p. 382.

4. Adams, *ibid.*, pp. 382–83

5. George Washington, 1783, cited in *The Writings of George Washington from Original Manuscript Sources*, 1745–99, J. C. Fitzpatrick, ed. (Washington, D.C.: U.S. Government Printing Office, 1931), vol. 26, p. 485

6. Ralph Waldo Emerson, *The Journals of Ralph Waldo Emerson*, Robert N. Linscott, ed. (New York: Random House, The Modern Library, 1960), p. 369

7. Alexis de Tocqueville, *Democracy in America*, The Henry Reeve Text, revised by Francis Bowen; Phillips Bradley, ed. (New York: Alfred A. Knopf, 1963), vol. II, p. 334

8. Henry Adams, *History of the United States During the Administrations of Jefferson and Madison*, George Dangerfield and Otey M. Scruggs, eds. (Englewood Cliffs, N.J.: Prentice-Hall, 1963), vol. II, ch. IV, pp. 172–73, 176, 182

9. Richard Hofstadter, *The American Political Tradition and the Men Who Made It* (New York: Alfred A. Knopf, 1973), p. 31

10. Thomas Jefferson, *Notes on Virginia* 1782, in *The Life and Selected Writings of Thomas Jefferson*, Adrienne Koch and

William Peden, eds. (N.Y.: Random House, The Modern Library, 1944), p. 280

11. Jefferson, Letter to William Short, November 28, 1814, *ibid.*, p. 654

12. Jefferson, Letter to John Melish, January 13, 1813, *ibid.*, p. 621

13. John Marshall, *The Life of George Washington* (Philadelphia: 1839), vol. II, p. 192; cited in Robert Faulkner, "John Marshall," in *American Political Thought*, Morton J. Frisch and Richard G. Stevens, eds. (New York: Charles Scribner's Sons, 1971), p. 76.

14. Sinclair Lewis, *Babbitt* (London: Jonathan Cape, 1960), p. 12

15. William Leggett, cited in Marvin Meyers, *The Jacksonian Persuasion* (Stanford, Calif.: Stanford University Press, 1960), p. 200

16. De Tocqueville, *ibid.*, vol. I, p. 290

17. Karl Marx, *The Poverty of Philosophy*, Second Observation, ii, 1, C. P. Dutt and V. Chattopadhyaya, eds. (New York: International Publishers, 1936), p. 92

18. De Tocqueville, *ibid.*, vol. I, p. 252

19. De Tocqueville, *ibid.*, vol. II, p. 257

20. De Tocqueville, *ibid.*, pp. 136–37

21. De Tocqueville, *ibid.*, pp. 318–19

22. J. Hector St. John Crèvecoeur, *Letters From an American Farmer 1782* (New York: Fox Duffield & Co., 1904), p. 61

23. Crèvecoeur, *ibid.*, pp. 61–66

24. De Tocqueville, *ibid.*, vol. II, p. 99

25. Abraham Lincoln, The First Inaugural Address, March 4, 1861, in *The Collected Works of Abraham Lincoln*, Roy P. Basler, ed. (New Brunswick, N.J.: Rutgers University Press, 1953), vol. IV, p. 271

26. Lincoln, Peoria, Illinois, October 16, 1854, *ibid.*, vol. II, p. 255

27. Thomas Paine, *Rights of Man* (London: Penguin Books, Ltd., 1969), pp. 186–87

28. Burke, *ibid.*, p. 149

CHAPTER SIX: CONSERVATIVE POLITICAL ECONOMY

Epigraph: Benjamin Disraeli, in a speech to the House of Commons April 25, 1843

1. Ronald Reagan, October 27, 1964

2. Reagan, Address to a Joint Session of Congress, February 15, 1981

3. Chief Justice Morrison R. Waite, *Munn* v. *Illinois*, 94 U.S. 113–126 (1876), p. 126

4. Thomas Aquinas, *The Summa Theologica of St. Thomas*

Aquinas, trans. by The Fathers of the English Dominican Province (New York: Benzinger, 1914), no. II, pt. II, question 58, art. 1

5. Charles de Gaulle, *War Memories: The Call to Honor 1940–1942* (New York: The Viking Press, 1955), p. 1
6. Woodrow Wilson, cited in Richard Hofstadter, *The American Political Tradition and the Men Who Made It* (New York: Alfred A. Knopf, 1973), p. 234
7. Hofstadter, *ibid.*, Introduction, pp. xxx–xxxi
8. James Madison, *The Federalist,* Jacob E. Cooke, ed. (Middletown, Conn.: Wesleyan University Press, 1961), No. 51, p. 349
9. Alexis de Tocqueville, *Democracy in America,* The Henry Reeve Text, rev. by Francis Bowen; Phillips Bradley, ed. (New York: Alfred A. Knopf, 1963), vol. II, p. 123
10. David Hume, "Of Commerce," *Philosophical Essays on Morals, Literature, and Politics,* First American Edition (Georgetown, D.C.: W. Duffy, 1817), p. 282
11. John Stuart Mill, Review of *Democracy in America* by Alexis de Tocqueville (*Edinburgh Reviews,* October, 1840), in *Essays on Politics and Culture,* Gertrude Himmelfarb, ed. (New York: Doubleday & Company, 1962), p. 248
12. Benjamin Disraeli, Speech to House of Commons, February 28, 1859
13. De Tocqueville, *ibid.,* p. 159
14. De Tocqueville, *ibid.,* vol. I, p. 416

CHAPTER SEVEN: ETERNITY WARNING TIME

Epigraph: Alexis de Tocqueville, *Democracy in America,* The Henry Reeve Text, rev. by Francis Bowen, Phillips Bradley, ed. (New York: Alfred A. Knopf, 1963), vol. II, p. 7

1. Plato, *The Republic,* viii, 545–46, trans. with introduction and notes by Francis MacDonald Cornfeld (New York: Oxford University Press, 1958), p. 2691
2. Edgar Allan Poe, "To Helen" (1831), st. I, 2, in *The Complete Tales and Poems of Edgar Allan Poe,* Hervey Allen, ed. (New York: Random House, Inc., The Modern Library, 1938), p. 1017
3. Robert Browning, "Paracelsus," pt. V, 742–43, on *The Works of Robert Browning,* Centenary Edition, F. G. Kenyon, C.B., ed. (London: Smith, Elder & Co., 1912), vol. I, p. 164
4. Father Ronald Knox, *The Belief of Catholics* (New York: Sheed and Ward, 1953), p. 6
5. John Milton, *Areopagitica,* John W. Hales, ed. (London: Oxford University Press, 1961), p. 44

6. Shakespeare, *Troilus and Cressida*, Jackson J. Campbell, ed. (New Haven: Yale University Press, 1959), I, iii, lines 83–85, 101–11, p. 23

7. August Kubizek, *The Young Hitler I Knew* (Boston: Houghton Mifflin Co., 1955), p. 84

8. De Tocqueville, *ibid.*, p. 98

9. Learned Hand, *The Spirit of Liberty*, Irving Dilliard, ed. (New York: Alfred A. Knopf, 1952), p. 77

10. Robert Peel, cited in Ian Gilmour, *Inside Right: A Study of Conservatism* (London: Hutchinson & Co., 1977), p. 9

11. Lord Balfour, from the Introduction to the English Constitution, *The Collected Works of Walter Bagehot* (London: Oxford University Press, World Classics Edition, 1952), p. xxii

12. Thomas Jefferson, in *The Life and Selected Writings of Thomas Jefferson*, Adrienne Koch and William Peden, eds. (Random House, The Modern Library, 1944), p. 277

13. Walter Lippmann, *The Public Philosophy* (New York: The New American Library, 1956), p. 95

14. Hand, *ibid.*, p. 118

15. Frederick L. Will, "The Rational Governance of Practice," *American Philosophical Quarterly*, vol. XVIII, No. III, July 1981, p. 192

16. Will, *ibid.*, p. 193

17. Will, "Reason, Social Practice, and Scientific Realism," *Philosophy of Science*, vol. 48, No. 1, March 1981, p. 8

18. Will, *ibid.*, p. 2

19. James Madison, *The Federalist*, Jacob E. Cooke, ed. (Middletown, Conn.: Wesleyan University Press, 1961), No. 56, p. 378

20. William James, *Memories and Studies* (New York: Longman, Green & Co., 1911), p. 58

21. T. S. Eliot, "Little Gidding," V, in *The Complete Poems and Plays 1909–1950* (New York: Harcourt, Brace & World, Inc., 1971), p. 145

22. George Santayana, *The Works of George Santayana* (New York, Charles Scribner's Sons, 1933), vol. IV, *The Life of Reason*, p. 132

Index